Praise for

Never stop writing, Adesuwa. Your hands are blessed
—Glory Abah, Bestselling Author

Adesuwa writes beautiful, authentic African characters.
—Amaka Azie, Bestselling Author

Adesuwa's characters get me talking to, laughing with, and crying with them.
—Feyi Aina, Bestselling Author

Adesuwa blows my mind every time I read her books.
—Mosunmola Rose, Bestselling Author

Adesuwa's pieces have never fallen short of exceptional.
—Mara Abutu, Bestselling Author

Adesuwa's writing is seamless and beautiful.
—Aminat Sanni-Kamal, Bestselling Author

Adesuwa never disappoints, never!
—Temitope Adeniran, Goodreads Reviewer

THE MARRIAGE CLASS

The Marriage Class

The Marriage Class © 2023 by Adesuwa O'Man Nwokedi

The right of Adesuwa O'Man Nwokedi to be identified as the author of this work has been asserted by her in accordance with the copyright laws.

All rights reserved. No part of this book may be used or reproduced or transmitted in any manner whatsoever without written permission of the copyright holder, except in the case of brief quotations embodied in critical articles or reviews.

This is a work of fiction. Names, places, events and incidents are either the products of the author's imagination or used fictitiously. Any resemblance to actual persons, living or dead, is purely coincidental. It is based in an ideal world where the COVID-19 pandemic totally didn't happen.

First Edition: February 2023

Acknowledgments

First of all, I would like to say a special thank you to my best friend and sounding board, Chichi Abiagam, for listening to all the million variations I have had for every story, picking all the holes I missed, reading re-write after re-write, and then again to check for grammar. I don't take your support for granted and I love you endlessly. Thank you for all you do!

I would also like to thank my beta readers, Orobosa Adenusi (my ride or die since the TFC days. I love you scatter), Toriola Adebisi, Stephanie Ozoemena, and Uche Anaekwe, for the structural critique. I appreciate it. Thank you, Uche, for helping with the Abi and Raymond storyline. Your observation was the very thing I needed to steer me in the right direction.

My appreciation also goes to early readers like Blessing Okwuofu (for catching every single *gbagaun*), Eunice Olasehinde, Temitope Adeniran, Ifunenya Isoje, and Chioma Jack. Thank you for always taking the time to read and promote my books. From the bottom of my heart, I appreciate it.

Thank you.

Dedication

To Onyeabor, who lets me hide in my writing cave for as long as I need to.

And to Carmen, Claire, and Benedict, who hover around while I do.

You are my everything!

1. OF LOVERS AND PROPOSALS

May 2022

It is 5:10pm and I know I need to be, at least, on Third Mainland Bridge by now, if I want to have any hope of making my appointment on time. But instead, here I am, unable to take my eyes off my damned screen, off this damned LinkedIn page, off the damned face of my ex-fiancé announcing his new role with one of the biggest banks in the country.

Lucas Oseghale Ibazebo – Vice President, Investor Relations

I glare at his smiling profile, at his toothy grin, and curl my upper lip. His teeth aren't this white, please. And his skin isn't this baby smooth either, what with the small scars he

THE MARRIAGE CLASS

got as souvenirs from adolescent acne and the bumps that have taken permanent residence around his jawline after he made the decision to go clean shaven. His photographer has clearly worked overtime to filter and retouch the image to perfection. Well, not too perfect, as I can still make out the small horizontal scar atop his right eyebrow. My eyes rove the picture, taking in other familiar details - the almost imperceptible asymmetry of his eyebrows with the right one not quite as thick as the left, the perfect ombré blend of brown and pink of his lips…and a lump forms in my throat.

God, I miss this man!

My eyes drop to his left hand, *that* finger and the shiny platinum wedding ring it brandishes, and I curse under my breath.

God, I hate this man!

I am scrolling down the page to read more about this new job of his, when there is a tap on my window. I look up to see my colleague, Ebiseme, standing on the other side of the glass partition, tapping her wrist with an arched brow.

Yes, I know I'm late.

"Abi, why are you still here? I thought you said your marriage class starts today."

I twirl the large diamond ring on my finger and curse when my eyes drop to the clock at the top corner of my screen. 5:29pm.

Shit!

Grabbing my laptop, I shove it into my messenger bag and gather my personal effects – phones, power bank, air pod case, and half-drunk bottle of water - from my table, throwing them into my Valentino handbag without the usual, almost pedantic, care to ensure everything is in the right place; phones in the small pocket just below the inner zip covering an even smaller pocket where the air pod case typically resides, and with the bottle of water securely fastened and standing in an upright position, to avoid any stories that touch the heart.

"It's on the mainland, isn't it?" Ebiseme seems hell bent on making me feel worse than I already do. "Are you sure you can make it? It's already past 5."

"I'll make it," I throw at her as I rush out of my office.

I sprint to the elevator, almost tripping over myself in my impractical five inch-heeled Roger Vivier pumps, barely entering the lift before the doors close, rushing out as soon as it opens on the ground floor. I shove past people in my haste to the car park and, once there, grab my phone and set the location on Google Maps. Fifty-five minutes to the location.

Shit! Shit!! Shit!!!

The class starts at 6pm and I'm going to be late…for the very first one.

THE MARRIAGE CLASS

I'm running late, my thumb flies across the keyboard of my phone. ***But I'll be there soon.***

Now, you see, the word *soon* is relative. Very relative.

Inhaling deeply, I cue on the car's sound system and my lips broaden into a smile when Wande Cole's *Iskaba* starts to play, my anxiety calmed and my jitters dispelled. So what, if this is the song that has been on repeat in my car for the past month? So what, if this is the one song guaranteed to make me happy? So what, if this is the song Lucas and I always listened to in his car? So what, if this song still reminds me of him?

None of that matters, right?

With the song on repeat, I navigate my way through Victoria Island traffic and, as it always happens every time I listen to it, my mind drifts to Lucas and, once again, I curse him for what he did to me. What he did to us.

The honking of more than a few cars jolts me out of my reverie. Looking up, I see that the traffic light has long gone green. A commercial bus overtakes me and the irate driver looks like he wants to stretch his hand into my car to give me a slap.

"All you women wey no fit drive! Go find driver jor!"

"Gerraway!" I yell back, rolling my eyes for emphasis. With a dismissive wave, I kick the car back into action and join the cars getting on the bridge.

ADESUWA O'MAN NWOKEDI

There is bumper-to-bumper traffic and by the time I drive into the church's parking lot in Yaba, it is already dark. Choosing a spot under an overhead light, as I park my car, I let out a loud sigh.

Am I really doing this?

A tap on my window makes me jump. I look up to see Raymond smiling at me. Lean, tall, and with the kind of suave good looks you would see in those late 1990s and early 2000s African American movies – with his sleepy eyes, dimpled smile, skin the colour of butterscotch, and a curly and soft beard neatly cropped and a testament to how seriously he takes grooming – Raymond is my fiancé. Smiling back at him, I turn the car off and disembark. In typical Raymond manner, he pulls me into a warm embrace, despite the fact I'm almost an hour late.

"Thank God. I was worried you wouldn't get here on time."

"There was a lot of traffic." It sounds weak even to me, but I don't offer more as I close my eyes and allow myself bask in the spicy notes of his perfume. If there is one thing I love about this man, this man I am about to marry, it is the way he smells. God, he smells so good.

"You look tired," he says, tipping up my chin. "Stunning, but tired."

I roll my eyes as he chuckles, pulling myself away from his embrace. "It's 7pm and I just finished fighting my way through rush hour traffic. So, duh, looking tired is a given, don't you think?"

He smiles and takes my hand. "All the more reason why you should have let me pick you up."

Still holding my hand, he leads me to a two-story building adjacent to the large building that houses the main church, and I try my best to keep up with his brisk pace. But while he seems eager to get to the class, my feet are lead-heavy with each step.

"Has the class started?" I ask as we walk up the dimly lit stairs.

"Only about five minutes ago. The Instructors wanted to wait for more couples to get here. There were only three of us here at 6pm when it was supposed to start."

"Why am I not surprised?" I scoff. "This place is in the middle of nowhere."

He laughs, not taking any offence at all. Typical Raymond.

"Yaba is very central, Miss I-Never-Leave-The-Island," he grins. "And, like I told you before, this is the only place I could find with a short enough program to allow us complete the course before our wedding date. Every other place, both our churches inclusive, have classes that run as long as six months."

The reminder of how close our nuptials are makes me stiffen.

We walk into a room on the second floor and are met by a smiling couple standing in front of the class. Attractive and middle-aged, possibly in their late forties or early fifties, they are the conveners of the class, from the look of things.

"Oh, great! Your fiancée has arrived," the woman says to Raymond while smiling at me. "Welcome."

I manage a stiff smile in response. As Raymond leads me to chairs in the middle row, my eyes scan the room, fascinated by the varied mix of people in the class.

The female convener waits for us to be seated before she resumes talking.

"For the benefit of those just joining us, we'll introduce ourselves again. My name is Ifeyinwa and this is my husband, Maxwell. We've been married twenty-six years and have coordinated St. Claire's marriage class for at least half that time."

Her voice drifts off as I continue to look around, more interested in the other couples than what the Ifeyinwa woman is saying.

Hmmm, so we're all here to do this thing *sha*.

As my eyes scan the room, I notice three women sitting unpaired; a young woman in her twenties, a pleasant-faced woman who looks about my age, and a woman who looks to be in her late thirties or early forties, but with an expertly made up face and buxom curves barely contained by the tight, low-cut dress she wears.

THE MARRIAGE CLASS

The door opens and a young man walks in. My eyes widen as he walks past the woman who looks closer his age, past the woman who looks my age, and heads, instead, to the older woman. My mouth drops in surprise as they exchange a brief kiss, eliminating any doubt that they are, indeed, a couple.

Omo, nothing we no go see for this Lagos!

The door opens again and an attractive middle-aged man walks in. He sits next to the woman who looks my age, shrugging her off as she tries to put her arm around him in welcome, and I am unable to help the snigger that escapes my mouth.

Raymond turns to me, the furrow of his brows showing his displeasure that I'm not listening to what the class conveners are saying. I frown at him and reluctantly return my attention to the front of the class. Ifeyinwa's husband is talking now.

"It looks like most of us are here," he is saying. "For the newcomers, my name is Maxwell, and Ifeyinwa, my wife, will repeat our introduction after the class. But for the sake of everyone else, we'll move forward to the part I love the most." A smile spreads across his face. "The getting- to-know-you-part."

Ifeyinwa is also smiling. "Basically, one member of each couple will make introductions on your behalf. You know, names, what you do for a living, how long you've been together, that kind of thing. And, to make it more interesting, the other person will tell us your proposal story."

I sigh deeply and shut my eyes. This is going to be a *looooong* evening.

A dark skinned woman raises her hand. Attractive, flashy, and flamboyant in a bright red jumpsuit with bold white vertical stripes and large diamante – or at least I hope they are diamante and not actual diamonds – chandelier earrings, she looks overdressed even to me.

"We'll go first," she giggles. "My name is Ewatomi, or Ewa to my eight hundred and seventy-six thousand followers on Instagram." She giggles again. "I'm twenty-eight years old and a fashion and beauty influencer."

I roll my eyes. Why am I not surprised she's *that* type?

"And this is my gorgeous fiancé, Sanya. He's a former model turned business mogul."

I scoff under my breath, my eyes moving to the guy who doesn't look a day older than thirty-five. Mogul indeed.

Ewa looks at him, still giggling. "We've been together two years, but, as you can see, he still gives me butterflies."

I roll my eyes again, feeling like I'm going to throw up.

Maxwell nods at them. "It's nice to meet you both. So, Sanya, will you do the honors and tell us your proposal story?

THE MARRIAGE CLASS

Sanya nods, grinning. "I proposed to her at the Madison Hotel. I rented one of their halls, had it decorated with large helium balloons, inflated hearts, rose petals on the floor, the works." Turning to Ewa, his smile broadens. "I knew I had to make it special. I mean, look at her. She's a goddess and deserves only the very best. So, I put together the most beautiful, the most romantic set up ever, and popped the question."

Ifeyinwa is grinning so wide, her eyes are crinkled shut. "Oh lovely! Was it a surprise?"

Madison Hotel - July 2021

Still standing in the hall and holding the ring box in one hand, Sanya glanced at his watch with the other, looking anything but pleased.

While he was waiting downstairs, Ewa was getting her make up done in one of the hotel rooms, looking at the pictures her friend, Yewande, was showing her on her phone, pictures of the hall where Sanya was waiting. Grabbing the phone from Yewande, Ewa frowned as she scrolled through herself, not happy at all with what she was seeing.

"I told him not to get red balloons. They're too cliché! I told him to pick black and pink. This looks too Valentine's Day! Is it too

late to change them? Can we call the decorator to make a switch?"

Yewande frowned. "Ewa, the balloons look fine. Everyone has been waiting in the hall for over an hour. Let's get this over and done with before they start to leave and we don't have enough people in the shot."

Ewa squinted at the screen.

"What colour is that God-awful shirt he is wearing anyway? Is it cream, champagne, or what? Won't it clash with my..."

Yewande groaned in her frustration. "Ewa, it won't clash with anything. He looks good, and so do you. We need go downstairs NOW."

Almost an hour later, Ewa finally walked into the decorated hall, her freshly manicured, scarlet-nailed hands covering her face in her feigned confusion, squealing in bogus surprise as Sanya dropped to his knee, holding a large engagement ring.

"Ewa, my love, my sunshine," he smiled up at her. "Will you marry me?"

Dissolving into well-rehearsed tears, she stole a glance across the room to make sure her friend and Sanya's assistant were capturing the moment, before rushing into his arms.

"Yes, yes, a million times yes!"

THE MARRIAGE CLASS

Ewa giggles. "Yes, it was. I wasn't expecting it at all."

As she flashes the massive rock on her hand, I realize I have seen her, and that ring, before. Ah, I remember now. Their hashtag, #CheersToTheWellingtons, has been trending online for a while. I wonder why I thought the guy was related to the other famous Wellington. He's cute though, even if he is prematurely balding.

Ifeyinwa nods at Ewa and Sanya, the smile still on her face. "Beautiful. Congratulations!" Her eyes move to the next couple and she smiles in anticipation.

A guy with an afro returns her smile. "Hi, I'm Boma. I'm thirty-four years old and I run my own Sports Supply Company." He turns to his equally smiling companion. "And this is the love of my life, April."

Ifeyinwa beams at them. "Such a nice name, April. Is that when you were born?"

April shakes her head, her forehead pinched in a slight frown.

"No, I was born in October."

I look at her, alongside everyone else in the class, waiting for the punch line, waiting for her to tell us the story behind her name, but she says nothing, the expression on her face as vacant as an empty bottle. My cheeks inflate and I purse my lips to keep the deep belly laughter from escaping, but I'm not quite successful as it spurts as a considerably audible grunt, prompting yet another glare from Raymond.

Boma's smile has now waned and he coughs nervously. "April is twenty-nine years old and she's a Personal Shopper."

Ifeyinwa nods and smiles. "And your proposal story?"

Boma and April exchange a glance, and she flushes as he chuckles.

Boma's Bedroom - March 2022

Enveloped in a cloud of endorphins as he descended from the mountain-peak high of yet another explosive orgasm, Boma turned to April, his hand propping his head, staring in worshipful adoration at the woman lying next to him.

"Where have you been all my life?"

April giggled as she traced his chin with her finger. "Waiting for you."

"Marry me," Boma said to her, his gaze not wavering.

THE MARRIAGE CLASS

Her eyes widened in her surprise and a large grin covered her face. Jubilant, she threw her hands round his neck and pulled him as they dissolved back into the sheets.

I frown as April and Boma exchange another glance. Jeez, how hard can it be to tell a proposal story?

"Ummm," is all April can manage, and I don't even try to stop my eye roll. They need to sit down and let the next couple talk.

Coming to her rescue, Boma puts his arm around his fiancée. "We had a moment when we both just knew."

Ifeyinwa smiles at them, obviously endeared. "That's so lovely. How long had you two been together at the time?"

April giggles. "Two months."

My mouth drops open as murmurs sound across the room. Two months? Honestly, these two belong in a circus.

"It's actually five months now," Boma cuts in, his smile now with a tautness that was not there before. "We've been engaged three months and our wedding isn't till August, so we'll have known each other eight months by the time we get married. When you know, you know."

Ifeyinwa's smile remains on her face. "No need to get defensive, Boma. I agree with you completely. When you know, you do know."

She turns to the next couple, and the sexy forty-something-year-old woman raises a brow at her companion, who nods at her in assent. Turning to Ifeyinwa, the woman smiles.

"Hi. My given name is Kristina, but everyone calls me Kris. I'm an art curator." Her smile deepens as she turns to her fiancé. "And this here is Bola. He's an artist and we've been together about a year."

Ifeyinwa places a hand over her chest, and smiles. "An art curator and an artist. How romantic! Did he propose in an art gallery, exhibition, or museum? Make my day and tell me it happened somewhere like that."

Bola chuckles. "Nothing quite so dramatic. I proposed over dinner."

Alcapone Italian Restaurant - February 2022

Kris and Bola walked hand-in-hand into the restaurant. Seeing some people she knew, Kris walked ahead to speak to them. As she walked away, Bola watched her with a smile on his face, drinking in the sight of her curvaceous body with all its contours gripped by the jersey fabric of her sleeveless black dress, her waist-long braids brushing her bottom. She turned to him and smiled when their eyes held. In response, he blew her a kiss and she looked away, laughing. He was still watching her as he took his seat, and as she walked back to their table minutes later.

Sitting down, she shook her head and chuckled. "I was trying to talk business. Why were you making me blush like a schoolgirl?"

He leaned forward. "I was just in awe of the fact that I'm the one who's lucky enough to be here with you tonight."

She rubbed her foot against his and winked at him. "In more ways than one."

"Seriously, babes. Every day, I wake up so grateful that, of everyone you could have picked, you picked me."

Her smile waned as her eyes held his, like she was searching for something. After looking at him for almost a clear minute, she shook her head.

"I've been waiting for the other shoe to drop, waiting for when you'll show me you're just like every other man, and that all this," *she gestured at the space between them,* "is just an act."

He raised a brow. "After almost a year? Really, Kris?"

She shrugged as she picked up the menu. "Let's order."

A waiter walked to their table and they placed their orders; a vegetarian lasagna for her and chicken piccata for him. As their food was served, they were soon back to flirting and laughing. They were enjoying their sticky toffee pudding dessert when a waiter walked up to them with a covered plate and set it before Kris.

"I didn't order more dessert," she said, looking from the waiter to Bola. "Or did you?"

Bola just smiled back at her, his eyes dancing.

Returning her attention to the covered plate, she lifted the metal cover and gasped at the sight of a white gold ring with a cushion-shaped diamond in an open black velvet box. Looking up at Bola, she gasped again when she saw him already on one knee.

"Bola!"

"You're the one, Kris," he answered. "You're the one I want to spend the rest of my life with."

She gaped at him for a while before bursting into laughter. "You're a comedian, you know that? Sit down and stop messing about."

As a frown creased his face, her laughter faded and she was awash with a mix of emotions, equal parts blown away...and concerned.

"Wait, you're serious?"

A small smile played on his lips. "As a heart attack."

She wanted to smack him up side his head, but she also found herself starting to hope.

"Are you sure? Bola, are you sure?"

"I've never been more certain of anything else in my life."

THE MARRIAGE CLASS

"Bola, this is marriage we're talking about," Kris prodded, her anxiety and excitement rising in equal measure. "This is a whole lot bigger than you and I just fooling around."

"You bet it is. And the last thing I've been doing with you is fooling around." He reached for her hand. "All I need right now is for you to say yes, Kris. Just say yes."

She regarded for him a while, before a slow smile curved her lips as she nodded. "Yes."

Bola's smile was as wide as his eyes. "Yes?"

Kris nodded again, tears in her eyes now. "Yes, you mad man. You're a lunatic, but yes!"

"A proposal over dinner. Classic and simple," Ifeyinwa remarks. "Congratulations."

As she turns to the next couple, my eyes remain on Kris and Bola, and to say I am fascinated would be an understatement. I can't get over how he is looking at her like she's a slice of hot bread with melted butter slathered all over, how they are looking at each other like they want to rip off their clothes and go at it right here and now.

This thing called love!

Following a prompting smile from Ifeyinwa, the next couple immediately takes their cue, and the guy, a dark skinned, devastatingly handsome man, smiles.

"My name is Ayokunle, but everyone calls me A.K. I'm an oil trader."

My brows raise, my interest piqued. In a sparkling white shirt I can immediately recognize as Tom Ford, with a cropped, well-manicured beard, small feminine-looking pink lips, a broad chest, and toned biceps, he is the perfect hybrid of smooth with a little bit rough. Not bad. Not bad at all.

My eyes travel to his fiancée and I do a double take when I behold the plain looking, borderline unattractive, woman. My eyes shoot back to A.K., who is looking at her with utter adoration, and it takes everything for me not to scratch my head in my bewilderment. That's whom he's engaged to? Her? With bulging eyes, thick lips, and a very pronounced overbite, she is nothing like what I would have expected a gorgeous man like him to consider appealing. From the way the other couples are either staring at them or exchanging glances, I can see I'm not the only astonished person in the room.

A.K., oblivious, is still smiling at the woman beside him. "This is Chioma, the lady I'll be lucky to soon call my wife. She works in aviation sales."

I roll my eyes. Aviation sales indeed! Fancy name for a Travel Agent.

Ifeyinwa turns to the Chioma, smiling in expectation, and Chioma smiles back, looking more than a little nervous.

"He proposed to me where it all began."

THE MARRIAGE CLASS

"Where you met?" Ifeyinwa asks.

"Where we fell in love," A.K. answers.

Epe Beach – January 2022

As A.K. and Chioma walked down the beach, as he talked animatedly, her eyes searched the eyes of everyone walking past them and, just like always, all she could do was wonder what they were thinking, certain they were puzzled that a man like him was with someone like her. Even with her friends and colleagues, as happy as they were for her, she caught their looks of wonder, amazement, and even bewilderment many times, all of them surprised she had caught the attention of the drop-dead-gorgeous Ayokunle Pierce. Seeing a group of women chatting in a group, she was so distracted by them that she wasn't focused when A.K. leaned in for a kiss.

"Are you okay?" he asked, his brows furrowed. "You've been very quiet tonight."

She shrugged and managed a strained smile. "I'm just tired. It was a really busy week."

"That's why I brought you here. To relax!" he said, pulling her in for a hug.

She tensed in his arms when she saw that the women were now looking in their direction. One of them waved.

"A.K! Ayokunle!" the woman yelled.

Turning in the direction of her voice, A.K. waved back, and Chioma pursed her lips, detaching herself from his hold. The strange woman left her group and ran over, her bouncy breasts bobbing up and down beneath a flimsy tank top, and her fleshy thighs flexing with each movement of her legs. The closer she got, the more perfect Chioma thought she looked, with spotless, glassy skin the colour of smooth caramel, and denim shorts cut so high, they could pass for briefs. Very skimpy briefs.

"Wow! A.K! Fancy seeing you here! It's been ages."

A.K. smiled and nodded. "It sure has. What are you doing here?"

The woman cocked her head to the side, still smiling. "Bachelorette Party." She touched his upper arm. "You look good."

He smiled and nodded. "Thanks. So do you."

They - all three of them - stood in awkward silence and the woman cast a look at Chioma, her brows raised, before smiling again at A.K.

"Don't be a stranger, okay?" she said to him. "Let's meet up for lunch sometime."

He smiled and the woman winked at him before sauntering away. When she was gone, Chioma hissed, turned around, and started walking back the way they came.

"Chioma! Chioma, where are you going?" A.K. called out, bewildered.

She didn't answer but instead quickened her pace. He ran to catch up with her.

"Chioma! Wait!"

She turned to face him, tears now pooled in her eyes. "I don't know which is more painful; you brazenly flirting with another woman, or you not even caring to introduce me."

"What are you talking about? Flirting with whom? I was just being polite."

"Polite to her but disrespectful to the person who is supposed to be your girlfriend? If you really didn't mean to disrespect me, you could have told her, point blank, that you can't have lunch with her because you're with someone else now!"

A.K. sighed, exasperated. "Of course I have no intention of meeting her for lunch, or anything else. Heck, I don't even remember who she is."

"Well, she definitely remembers you."

Sighing deeply, he shook his head and palmed his face. "Chioma, that was why I didn't introduce you. I have no clue who she is, let alone remember her name. We've gone through this before, babes. You know I have a past..."

"You don't say!"

"Sarcasm doesn't become you, my beloved," he chuckled, reaching for her hands.

But she wasn't at all amused.

"What are you even doing with me, A.K.?" she sighed, shaking her head as she also pondered the same question. *"Everywhere we go, people stare at us like the very oddity we are, I'm sure wondering whether you are under some sort of spell impairing your judgment."*

"I don't care what people wonder or think, Chioma. You're the best thing that has ever happened to me."

She rolled her eyes and turned around, continuing to walk in the direction of the hotel.

"Did I say something wrong?" A.K. called.

"A.K., please, I can't deal," she shouted back, not even looking at him. *"I'm not strong enough to handle the heartbreak that is warming up for me ahead, the heartbreak that will come when you go from sweet-talking me to no longer taking my calls. It's better for me to save myself while I still can. I know how these things go, and, to be honest, I'm surprised I've allowed myself get carried away for this long."*

"Chioma!" he yelled her name again, but she waved her hand in dismissal. "Chioma!" he called out louder.

The urgency in his voice made her turn around to look at him, and she gasped upon seeing him on one knee, holding a ring.

"I was going to do this further down the beach. I've already set up a cabana with candles, flowers, and wine."

Her lips parted as she gaped at him. "A.K., what are you doing?"

THE MARRIAGE CLASS

"I love you more than anything, Chioma. You're the one my heart has been waiting for. Marry me...please."

Her tears returned, but they were happy tears now. "A.K., don't joke with something like this."

He smiled at her. "Does it look like I'm joking? I love you, Chioma Nkadi, and I want nothing more than to spend the rest of my life with you."

Overcome with emotion, she ran to him, dropped to her knees and wrapped her arms around him, their lips connecting in a passionate kiss.

"It was an impromptu proposal along the beach," Chioma smiles, her eyes dilated in her state of reminisce. "We eventually made it to the cabana he'd set up, and it was just as beautiful as he'd told me it was, if not even more so."

Ifeyinwa, grins. "I hope you made him repeat it there."

Chioma turns to a beaming A.K. "He didn't have to. I would have said yes even if he'd proposed to me in the middle of Balogun Market."

I palm my face and shake my head. Somebody save me now!

Ifeyinwa turns to the next couple, and a well-dressed woman in a bright purple blouse, who looks to be in her late thirties, smiles at her. Her partner, a man in his early forties, is wearing sunglasses, even though we are indoors and it is now nighttime.

"Hi, there. I just have to say, I love your blouse. Is it satin?" Ifeyinwa gushes.

The woman smiles, obviously pleased someone has noticed her expensive attire.

"Thank you. It's silk." She throws an awkward glance at her partner, who smiles at her. Shrugging, she returns her gaze to Ifeyinwa. "I'm Ogechi and a Senior Vice President with Avalon Investment Bank. My fiancé's name is Chizulukeme, or Zulu as everyone calls him. He's a businessman."

Ifeyinwa nods with interest. "And how long have you been together?"

Ogechi smiles and her face flushes. "Only a little longer than that couple over there." She looks in the direction of Boma and April, and Ifeyinwa nods in understanding.

"And what was your proposal like?" Ifeyinwa directs this question at Zulu.

Zulu clears his throat and answers in a heavily Igbo-accented voice. "Will it be okay if she answers for us?"

Ogechi purses her lips, irritation flashing quickly across her face, before she forces a smile. "There wasn't any proposal, per say. We're both people of a certain age, and we just knew, I guess." She nods in Boma's direction again. "Just like he said, when you know, you know."

Victoria Island - March 2022

Ogechi walked out of her office building and frowned at the ostentatious black Escalade parked right in front of it. The window slid down and Zulu grinned at her.

"Achal'ugo nwanyi! You look beautiful as always. Biko, enter the car before the sun toasts this your lovely skin."

The driver walked around the car to lead Ogechi to the back passenger seat, and she frowned before reluctantly following him. Getting into the back seat next to Zulu, she turned to glare at him.

"I didn't know you were coming with a driver. When you asked me not to drive to work today, I thought you were going to come alone."

Zulu chuckled. "Baby, is that why you have spoilt your face with that frown? Why will I want to drive myself in this traffic, when I'm not crazy? Why would I want to get where we're going frustrated? Nne, this life na only one."

Ogechi pursed her lips and looked ahead. The date hadn't even started but she'd just about had enough. Zulu touched her hand, startling her, and prompting a chuckle from him.

"This one you're so jumpy today. It's like you haven't eaten. What you need is to swallow some hot pounded yam and drink a sweating glass of cold malt drink. That will make your body calm down."

She turned to him, her eyes wide in her horror. "I hope you're not taking me back to that awful place. Absolutely not, if that's your plan. Let's go to Ricardo's, please. At least, I know what to expect from their menu."

"Ogechi, I'm begging you in the name of God. I still haven't recovered from that restaurant you made us go to on Sunday. In fact, I'm still purging."

She was unable to mask her disgust, and instead turned her head, no longer able to look at him.

Zulu continued to talk, oblivious. "The food was not only terrible for my stomach but also my pocket. Imagine paying over thirty thousand naira to eat rice…ordinary rice." He chuckled in his driver's direction. "Did you hear that, Osita? Ordinary rice and stew, thirty-four thousand naira! By the time they added her food and all their taxes, nna, the thing was almost seventy grand for two people. Is that not your one-month's salary? On top food!"

The driver chuckled in response, further annoying Ogechi.

"It wasn't just 'rice and stew'. It was a steak and rice pilaf dish!"

"Rice pi-gini? No be only pi-laugh, na pi-frown!" Zulu laughed heartily at his joke, joined by his chauffer. "Please, let's go and eat real food this time."

THE MARRIAGE CLASS

Her phone vibrated and she retrieved it from her bag, a huge frown still on her face as she wondered what she was doing with such an uncouth man.

Babes, don't forget what we discussed. Keep an open mind.

She frowned as she read and re-read the text from her older sister, Amaka. She turned to look at Zulu, who was now also scrolling through his phone. With a deep sigh, she threw her phone back into her handbag, just as they pulled up in front of an Efik restaurant. The driver helped her out of the car as Zulu disembarked from his side.

Ogechi's irritation returned as they walked into the packed restaurant, as people brushed past her, and as Zulu loudly greeted almost everyone they walked by. Once seated at a table, she perched precariously on the edge of her chair, not even making any attempt to get comfortable.

Zulu smiled at her. "Achal'ugo, what will you eat? You had egusi last time, abi? You should try their afang soup. It's so delicious, you'll want to eat your plate with the food."

Ogechi shook her head in her disinterest, reaching for her phone. "Thanks, but no thanks. I'll eat something when I get home."

"Baby, mba nau. How can you expect me to eat if you don't? They have rice here as well. Do you want jollof rice? Fried rice?"

"Nothing."

She started to type a reply to her sister's text. **I can't open my mind any more than I already have. This thing is not working...**

Zulu sighed, just as a waiter walked up to their table. "My brother, thank you. But we'll be leaving now."

Ogechi looked up from her phone, surprised, and Zulu smiled at her.

"Let's go where you want to eat. I will make sure I drink something to calm my stomach afterwards."

"Oh no, we don't have to leave," *she said, suddenly overcome with guilt, before turning to the waiter.* " I'll have some rice and vegetable sauce, please."

The waiter arched his brow, confused. "Rice and edikang ikong?"

Zulu chuckled, just as his phone started to ring. "Yes, my guy. Rice and edikang ikong. As for me, I'll have my usual."

As he answered his phone, Ogechi studied him, frowning as she looked at him from head to toe, from his box haircut, to his gold chain and bracelets, to his paisley patterned shirt, to his maroon trousers and black patent leather boots, none of which she found appealing. Their eyes met and he grinned at her. She could only respond with a stiff smile. Thankfully, he was distracted by another phone call, and she exhaled as she looked away, unsure how much longer she could pretend to want to be there.

Right about then, a heavily pregnant woman walked up to their table, a wide smile on her face.

"Sister Ogechi!"

The sound of the title made even Zulu look up from his call.

THE MARRIAGE CLASS

"Oh, hello," Ogechi answered, looking up at the woman. "Nwanne, right?"

The Nwanne squealed and bent to embrace her, not minding her large bump.

"Sis, you look so good!" Nwanne raved. "You look even younger than the last time I saw you." She giggled. "You're practically aging backwards. Anyone seeing us together would think I was the one older by almost ten years, and not you."

Ogechi's smile waned as she gently pulled away from the embrace. "Congratulations. It's good to see you. Is this your first?"

"My first is eight years old oh, sis. This one is my third and final. My last bus-stop, as I've told my husband." Nwanne glanced at Zulu, who was still talking on his phone, and she winked at Ogechi before bending to embrace her again. "I have to run. Please, extend my greetings to Uju." Then, in a whisper, added. "And please, make sure you invite me for the wedding. God has finally heard our prayers!"

As Nwanne rushed off, Ogechi stared at her wistfully, remembering her visiting their Enugu home, her eyes always wide with awe and admiration, her desire to be like them – Uju's older sisters – evident in everything she did and said. How ironic that now, she was the one whom Ogechi would give anything to be like! Sighing, Ogechi picked up her phone and deleted the text she'd been typing as a reply to Amaka's.

"My dear, no vex," Zulu said, his call now over. "These my boys sometimes behave like they have akamu in their brains!" Turning his phone face down, he grinned at her. "I promise, no more phone calls."

Ogechi smiled and nodded in understanding, seeing him in a new light. Maybe she could learn to tolerate him after all. He looked in the direction of the door.

"Was that your friend?"

She shrugged. "My younger sister's friend."

"Which of them? Amaka?"

Ogechi smiled, impressed he remembered her sister's name, albeit the wrong one.

"Amaka is my older sister. Uju is the youngest, the one in London. Nkechi, the one after me, is the one you spoke to over the weekend."

"The one who just turned thirty-five, right?" When she nodded, he smiled. "I look forward to meeting them."

Ogechi nodded but his smile waned as his eyes held hers.

"I'm serious, Achal'ugo. I want to meet them. I want to meet your entire family." He paused for a few seconds. "Your dad especially."

She nodded again, the implication of his words not lost on her. An Igbo man asking to meet a girl's father was the strongest declaration of his intentions that he could make. As their meals were served, Ogechi had flashbacks, flashbacks of the pregnant Nwanne from minutes before, flashbacks of posing for pictures as *a bridesmaid at all her sisters', and several friends', weddings, and she knew she would be a fool to pass up this opportunity that had finally presented itself after several years of waiting.*

Smiling at Zulu, she nodded. "I'd like that."

Maxwell smiles and nods. "A discussion is just as good a proposal as any. Congratulations."

He turns to the twenty-something-year-old woman sitting alone, who offers a shy smile back.

"Your fiancé couldn't make it today?" Maxwell asks.

"He's in Canada and taking his classes there, while I have mine here."

Maxwell nods in understanding. "I see. We've had a few couples like that before." Smiling at her, he shrugs. "Well, I guess you'll have to do the intro *and* tell your proposal story."

The young woman smiles and clears her throat, looking around nervously. "Well, I'm Bianca. I graduated from the University of Lagos last year and just finished my Youth Service." She laughs. "I'm also job-hunting, in case anyone here is hiring."

When nobody laughs, she clears her throat again.

"My fiancé's name is Prince, and he's a Project Management Specialist based in Toronto. We've been together about two years."

"And how did he propose?" Maxwell asks.

Bianca shrugs and smiles, even though her smile isn't quite as bright as before. "There was no real proposal, per say. Like the last couple, we just, you know, agreed. From the very beginning, we knew that was where our relationship was headed."

"Have you even met the guy?" Ewa asks from where she sits in the front row.

Sanya glares at his fiancée for her intrusion, but everyone else in the class has their eyes on Bianca, waiting for an answer. I, for one, am all-ears. A mail order bride? In 2022?

"No. Not yet. He was supposed to. He couldn't get away from work. We tried several times, but it couldn't happen."

Surulere - May 2021

Bianca rushed into her bedroom from the bathroom to answer her ringing phone, soapsuds still on her body, slipping on the smooth linoleum covered floor and almost falling in the process.

THE MARRIAGE CLASS

Grabbing the ringing device, she tapped the receive *button and Prince's face appeared on the screen.*

"Babe, where have you been?" he asked. "I've been calling you."

"I'm so sorry. I was in the bathroom. Look at my body, it's still covered in soap."

He grinned. "Your beautiful body that I can't wait to see…and hold."

Bianca smiled as she sat on the bed, reaching for another towel to wipe off the wayward bubbles.

"Any luck from the Department of Home Affairs? Will you still be able to make it home in June?"

He sighed and shook his head. "I was advised it would be best to submit a brand new application for my P.R. So, I'll have to start the process all over again."

Bianca sighed and looked at the pictures of her long-distance boyfriend taped to her mirror. "I was really looking forward to finally meeting you this time. It would have been so nice to see you face-to-face, instead of all these video calls." She laughed, but was so pained, it sounded more like a whimper. "I was looking forward to knowing what you smell like."

"It's just a delay, my love. But it's going to happen. I promise you. I'm not going to rest until this issue with my residency is resolved."

"But what if they reject your application again? What if they deport you?"

He chuckled. "Then we'll get to meet each other quicker."

"That's not even a little bit funny," she hissed. "Hang on while I get dressed."

She placed the phone on the bed, and rose to her feet.

"You know you could let me watch, right?"

She laughed as she got into her nightgown. "Pervert! There's no way I'm going to show you my goods via video chat. What incentive will you have to come home?"

"Trust me, plenty!"

Fully dressed, she picked up the phone again.

"I spoke with your mom today," she said. "She sounded much better than the last time we spoke on Sunday."

He winced. "I forgot to call her. I just got off work and only have a few minutes before I have to head to the factory.

"When are you going to have the time to complete your certification exam if you're still juggling all these jobs?"

"If I get the marketing job I told you about, I'll dump the others. It pays more than both of them combined.

"What about tutoring those Nigerian kids? Will you quit that too?"

"I can do that in my sleep," he scoffed. "I don't have to quit. It's easy income. Babe, I want to be so sorted that by the time you get here, you'll live a life of luxury. You won't even have to lift a finger."

"I hear you."

They were quiet for a few seconds.

"I better let you go," she finally said. "You'll be late if you don't head out now."

"I'll call you just before I clock in. Try not to fall asleep."

She managed to laugh. "I'll try."

He hesitated for a bit. "I'm sending you a link right now. Have a look at it and let me know what you think."

"A link for what?"

But the line disconnected.

Sitting back in her bed, her phone vibrated almost immediately. It was a message from Prince, with a link. Clicking it open, it led to a page with several engagement rings in different shapes and sizes displayed. She gasped, squealing as she hopped off the bed, wrapping both arms around her body as she shimmied in her glee. Her phone soon started to ring, and she rushed to answer it.

A smiling Prince showed on her screen. "Have you seen it?"

"Why are you asking me to look at engagement rings, Obiora Prince Mgbonu?"

The grin on his face grew wider. "Why else? It's about time, isn't it?"

She could only grin back at the phone, completely lost for words.

"We'll get you a better ring when you get here, I promise."

"You don't even have to. These ones are beautiful."

"Babe, you haven't even looked at them," he chuckled.

"I'll look...and I'll pick one."

"I'll send the ring you choose through a friend of mine coming to Lagos at the end of the month. Make sure you always wear it, okay? I want those Lagos boys to know you're taken."

She laughed, the wide smile on her face threatening to split her cheeks in half. "I'll never take it off."

He smiled and blew her a kiss. "You are the love of my life, Bianca. Thank you for making me the luckiest man alive."

"He is the love of my life, and I'm his. We might not have met each other physically, but he's my soulmate." Bianca shrugs, still smiling. "With these things, the heart always knows."

The last part of her statement hits me like a bullet. *The heart always knows.* I shut my eyes, assaulted by flashbacks I would much rather permanently forget.

THE MARRIAGE CLASS

Ikeja – June 2019

Lucas cupped my face as we sat in the living room of the flat he shared with his friend, his gaze deep and penetrating.

"You're the love of my life, Abi. I want nothing more than to spend the rest of my life with you. You're my soulmate."

I smiled at him, the man I loved with an intensity that scared me. "You always say that, but how do you know? How do you know that, of the billions of women in the world, I'm your soulmate?"

His gaze was unwavering. "The heart always knows."

And then he took my mouth in a deep, passionate kiss.

St. Patrick's Catholic Church, Maryland – April 2020

I stood next to my sister, Joyce, during Sunday Mass, singing a hymn from the weekly bulletin. As we sang, my eyes travelled across the page towards the marriage bans, and I gasped when I sighted it.

For the SECOND CALL, banns of marriage between Beverly Omoyeme Osime from Uromi, Edo State and Lucas Oseghale Ibazebo from Irua, Edo State.

My hands shook as the bulletin dropped from my hand. Joyce looked at me, concerned, before reaching for the bulletin now on the floor. As she gasped upon seeing the notice, I sat down, still in a daze.

My world shattered.

"Helloooo!"

I am jolted out of my reverie by Ifeyinwa's call, and I stare at her, blank for a few seconds before realization sets in.

"Oh, it's our turn? Okay, umm, my name is Abi, and I'm a banker." I turn to Raymond. "And this is my fiancé, Lucas…"

I grimace as I immediately realize my mistake.

Raymond smiles at Ifeyinwa. "Otherwise known as Raymond. I'm a Graphic Designer."

Ifeyinwa looks from me to Raymond, and back to me, confused.

"His name is Raymond, I'm sorry," I say, casting a plaintive look at him and he smiles back in reassurance. "And he was just being modest about being a Graphic Designer," I continue, desperate to make up for my goof. "He's one of the most brilliant animators in the country. As a matter of fact, in 2016, his short film was nominated for an Annie Award."

Ifeyinwa nods, her brows creased. "That's good to know. And how long have you been together?"

I turn to Raymond, suddenly blank. "Ummm…."

"Fifteen months," Raymond answers for me, smiling. "Not quite a whirlwind romance, but not a long one either. And we got engaged on my birthday." He puts his arm around my shoulder. "She planned a surprise birthday dinner for me, when I was the one with the surprise for her."

Les Frites Restaurant - March 2022

Raymond and I walked into the restaurant and about twenty of our friends already seated at a table decorated with black and gold helium balloons, yelled in unison, "SURPRISE!"

Raymond laughed and shook his head, pulling me into an embrace, overwhelmed by the gesture. As we kissed, our guests cheered. But as we took our seats, my mind flashed back to my birthday a few years before.

Alfredo's Restaurant - May 2019

I squealed in surprise as a group of my friends yelled "HAPPY BIRTHDAY!" I turned to the man by my side, Lucas, overwhelmed with emotion, and he tipped up my chin and kissed me.

"Happy thirtieth birthday, my love."

ADESUWA O'MAN NWOKEDI

Les Frites Restaurant - March 2022

Raymond was smiling before a well-lit birthday cake, still chuckling from his surprise.

"Gosh, I'm not one to ever get surprised, but you got me. You guys got me." He turned to me, shook his head and smiled. "You got me real good. How did you plan this without me having a clue? And it's not even a landmark birthday or anything."

"You deserve it, Raymond!" a guest chimed.

"You're always thinking of everyone else. You deserve to be the one on the receiving end for a change!" another said.

Raymond smiled at the guests, before turning again to me. His smile waned as his gaze held mine.

"Don't forget to make a wish," yet another guest called out.

Raymond's smile returned as he looked briefly at his cake, before returning his attention to me. "It was around this time a year ago that my life changed forever. I met the love of my life and I finally was able to understand just how deep and intense love can be. Not a day goes by without my thanking God for bringing you my way, Abi, and I want nothing more than to spend the rest of my life with you by my side."

Then, without warning, he got down on one knee, prompting a gasp from the entire room. He reached into his pocket.

"I was going to do this tonight anyway. I was going to do this even when I thought it would be just you and I here for dinner."

THE MARRIAGE CLASS

My eyes were wide as I gaped at him, speechless.

The Mandarin Hotel – July 2019

In a dimly lit deluxe room at the popular five-star hotel, surrounded by dozens of tea light candles and rose petals, Lucas got down on one knee, holding up a ring.

"Abieyuwa, my love, my life. You are the very air I breathe. Will you do me the honour of becoming my wife?"

In tears, I nodded, my joy indescribable, prompting a chuckle from him.

"You're going to have to answer me with words, darling."

"YES! In every language on God's green earth, yes! Yes, Lucas! Yes, I'll marry you."

Les Frites Restaurant – March 2022

I was staring at Raymond, frozen to the spot.

"Awww, she's at a complete loss for words!" a guest laughed.

Raymond's eyes were questioning as they held mine. "What do you say, babes? Will you ride this journey of life with me?"

I finally smiled and nodded. "Yes, Raymond, I'll be happy to."

We embraced, and as our guests broke into rapturous applause, he slipped the ring on my finger.

Raymond squeezes my shoulder, still smiling at Ifeyinwa. "That was the best day of my life, and I'm so excited at the prospect of doing life with her."

Ifeyinwa is smiling at us, the concern on her face no longer there. "That's beautiful. Congratulations."

As she turns to the next couple, Raymond smiles at me but I keep my eyes averted, not looking at him at all, ashamed of my slip…and hating that my excitement for our wedding is diminishing a little more with each passing day.

Ifeyinwa turns to the middle-aged man who walked into the class shortly after I did. Good looking in a brooding kind of way, he arches his brow.

"Come on, now. And there I was thinking this whole intro was for the young ones," he chuckles.

Ifeyinwa laughs and exchanges a glance with her husband before turning again to the man. "In this class, we don't see age. Only love." She smiles at his companion. "And for you to be here, then you definitely have a story for us."

The man shrugs. "Well, my name is Eric and I'm a businessman in the Fintech space." He nods in the direction of his fiancée. "And this is Ivie, the person who has dragged me here with a noose around my neck."

THE MARRIAGE CLASS

Ifeyinwa's eyes dart to Ivie's, but Ivie simply laughs in response to Eric's joke, or at least I hope it's a joke.

Maxwell clears his throat and cuts in, seeing that his wife is flummoxed. "And how did you two get here? What's your proposal story?"

Eric chuckles. "Does an ultimatum count as a 'proposal story'?"

There is a grunt from the next pew, and Eric turns around to see a man in his late thirties, chuckling. Eric laughs again.

"You see? He gets it!"

"Do I ever!" the man on the next pew chortles.

The chortling man's fiancée glares at him, but he continues to laugh along with Eric. Eric turns to look at the last couple, a bespectacled man and his very pregnant fiancée, and his laughter continues.

"I'll bet that's another guy who understands the meaning of the word 'ultimatum'."

The bespectacled man's eyes widen behind his glasses and he quickly looks away, just as his fiancée draws out a long hiss.

Landmark Events Center – February 2022

Eric and Ivie were seated in the lavishly decorated hall, for his friend's wedding reception. With over five hundred people in attendance, it was so well organized, it still created the illusion of an intimate ceremony – if a party with over five hundred people could be considered 'intimate'. With her arm interlinked with Eric's, Ivie leaned closer to whisper in his ear.

"You're the only one who hasn't complimented me today."

He glanced at her, bemused. "For?"

She giggled. "For how lovely I look, silly."

He looked at her, as if seeing her for the first time. "It's a pretty outfit. I'd know, since I bought it."

"You can't compare the way a dress looks on a hangar to how it looks on a woman." She nudged his shoulder with hers. "Your woman."

He smiled and shook his head. "You look beautiful, Ivie. You don't need me to tell you that."

Her smile waned. "I don't need it. I just want it."

He reached for his glass of champagne and took a sip, just as Timi Dakolo's *Iyawo Mi* started playing and the new couple took to center stage for their first dance. Eric chuckled and shook his head.

"Olumide is a fool to be doing this again."

Ivie turned to look at him. "Why is he a fool for wanting to spend forever with the woman he loves?"

Eric rolled his eyes. "A second time? He should have learned his lesson the first time around." He shook his head. "I wish someone had given me good advice when I was taking the plunge my second time. You've done one rodeo, you've done them all."

He took another sip of his drink just as Ivie pulled away from him, her countenance no longer bright and cheerful. He remained oblivious to her mood change as he bantered with people who walked by their table, and as he continued to answer calls on his phone.

"So, what are you saying?" she asked, several minutes later. "That you're done with the 'rodeo', as you call it?"

Eric didn't even turn to look at her.

"If you mean me being done with marriage, then hell yeah! I don't have to fail at something three times. Twice is more than enough."

She turned to watch the dancing couple, struggling not to give in to her tears. "So, what are we doing then? If marriage isn't a consideration, what are you doing with me?"

He groaned and turned to look at her. "Are you serious? You want to have this discussion here?"

She glared at him. "Why not here? You're always avoiding the topic. Why not here?"

"You couldn't have picked a worse place to be a brat, Ivie," he retorted, by now also irritated.

Her eyes widened before they narrowed into slits, in her rising rage. Reaching for her handbag, she rose to her feet.

"And where do you think you're going?" Eric demanded.

She didn't answer and instead brushed past him as she walked away. He remained sitting for a few minutes, rapping his fingers on the table to curb his vexation. Grunting, he finally rose and made his way out of the hall. Outside, he saw her standing on the road, glancing from her phone to oncoming traffic, as if waiting for something or someone.

"Of all the childish and juvenile things to do, this takes the cake," he muttered.

"Oh, I'm childish and juvenile now?"

"Yes! Do you know how silly you look, standing on the road in a dress like that, trying to flag a cab?"

"I'm not trying to 'flag' a cab. I've already ordered one on my app, and it'll be here any minute."

Eric groaned and covered his eyes with his hand. "Oh God! Why are you acting like a kid, Ivie? You're thirty-five years old and too old for this."

She turned to face him, her face a mask of rage. "Exactly! I'm way too old for you to waste any more of my life. We've been together three years..."

Eric threw his hands up in exasperation. "And long enough for you to know that marriage is not for me. I've done it twice already. My kids are grown. Why on earth would I want to do it again? You know this. I've never hidden the fact that commitment is the last thing I want, and I thought you were open-minded enough to accept that."

They stood there on the road as wedding guests walked and drove past them, not saying anything to each other for several minutes.

As her eyes pooled with tears, she shrugged. "Well, I guess I'm not open-minded enough after all."

"What does that even mean?"

She clenched her jaw and looked away, before turning back to him.

"It means I'm not doing this anymore, Eric. It means I'm done. I've tolerated your emotional cluelessness and expressive deficiencies, but I will not tolerate being a glorified bed warmer for the rest of my life."

An Uber pulled up in front of them and the driver wound down his window. "Ivie?"

She nodded at him before turning to glare at Eric again. "I'll come for my things during the week."

Eric looked on as she got into the car and as it drove off. Shaking his head, he put his hands in his pockets and blew out a puff of air.

Eric shrugged. "I didn't want to lose her, so I had to do what I had to do."

Maxwell turns to Ivie and she smiles at him, interlinking her arm with Eric's.

"He just needed a little nudge," she grins.

"Well then, congratulations," Maxwell smiles at her. "And welcome to our class."

I chuckle as I watch them. These ones don enter one chance!

Maxwell clears his throat and turns to the mouthy man seated behind Eric, his smile more sardonic than pleasant. "You seemed to have quite a bit to say earlier."

The mouthy man's fiancée leans forward. "I'll make our introductions. My name is…"

Maxwell raises his hand, his eyes still on the guy and the sardonic smile still on his face. "Please indulge me. I'd really like to hear from…"

There is a visible clench of the mouthy man's jaw. "Itse. My name is Itse. Spelt I.T.S.E and pronounced *eee-sh-eh*."

THE MARRIAGE CLASS

Maxwell nods, still smiling. "I'd really like to hear from Itse, pronounced *eee-sh-eh*, if that's okay with you both."

Itse and his fiancée exchange a glance. From the way she glares at him, she is still furious about his slip earlier.

"Like I just said, my name is Itse. My fiancée's name is Omasan, and we're both medical doctors."

Maxwell lets out a whistle. "Both medical doctors? How about that! Was that how you met?"

Itse finally smiles as he nods. "Yeah, we met in our first year of med school."

Maxwell crosses his arms, his brows raised in interest. "First year of med school? Sounds like a long time!"

"Nineteen years," Omasan says.

There is an unmissable edge in her voice.

Itse chuckles. "So, I guess you can say that us ending up here," he gestures around the room, "was inevitable."

MM2 Domestic Airport – January 2022

Omasan walked out, dragging a trolley-box behind her, ignoring calls from touts and taxi drivers. Looking around the car park, her large sunglasses did little to mask her irritation, her knotted brows and flared nostrils the dead giveaway to that fact. The honk of a car made her turn, and Itse, in the driver's seat of a Toyota Highlander, wove her over. Dragging her box to the other side of the road, she got into the car.

"Talk about the nick of time!" Itse chuckled, smiling at her as she buckled her seatbelt. "There was so much traffic, I was worried I'd get here late. These countless road constructions are a problem, I swear."

"Well, thank God you didn't get here late then," she muttered.

"You okay?"

She shrugged. "Just tired. Can we go?"

A wry smile formed on his face and he leaned into her. "Too tired for a kiss, after being separated the whole weekend?"

She hesitated briefly before turning to him. He smiled as he lifted her sunglasses, before covering her lips with his, savouring their taste like he hadn't been doing exactly that for almost two decades.

"Babes, let's go," she said, pulling back. "After the weekend I had, I need to rest."

He nodded and navigated the car out unto the road.

"How did it go with the Christening? I hope Misan wasn't too stressed," he said, as they coursed along the Oshodi-Apapa expressway.

THE MARRIAGE CLASS

Omasan shrugged. "The Christening went well. Everything went well."

She closed her eyes and he returned his attention to the road. A little over thirty minutes later, they were walking into their Yaba apartment, with him pulling her trolley-box behind him. He glanced at his watch.

"Do you want me to order anything for dinner? There's still time for us to eat together before I have to leave for the hospital."

She turned to look at him, a brow raised. "I thought you were on call this weekend."

"Rotimi asked me to cover for him tonight. I mentioned it to you when we spoke this morning."

She shook her head. "No, you didn't."

"Yes, I did. But why is that a big deal? Rotimi and I cover for each other all the time."

Omasan wove a dismissive hand as she walked away. "Do what you want. I'm too tired to argue."

Itse stared, confused, before walking after her.

"What is the problem, Omasan?" he demanded, entering their bedroom behind her. "If I cover for Rotimi tonight, it means I get to be free on Friday night for a change. Not all of us have the kind of flexible schedule you do."

asd"So, is that the issue now?" *she scoffed, her back to him as she dropped her handbag on the bed.* "The fact that I get to pick and choose my work hours and you don't?"

He stared at her back, flabbergasted, before raising his hands in surrender. "You're clearly spoiling for a fight, but babes, I'm not here for it. Whatever it is I've said or done to annoy you, I'm sorry, abeg. Let me order what it is you're eating for dinner and leave you to sleep off this crabbiness you've returned from Benin with."

"Everyone, every single person, that came for the Christening - from my aunties, to my uncles, to my cousins, to my childhood friends, to even my neighbours and their dog - everyone wanted to know why we're not married yet," *she threw at him as he turned around to leave.*

He turned back to her, completely knocked for six. "Huh?"

She glared at him. "You heard me."

"I don die!" *he chuckled, his hands on his waist.* "Wasn't it your sister's baby's Christening? Why was your own marital status of interest to anyone?"

"Because Misan is my younger sister! Because you and I have been together almost as long as she's been alive!"

Sighing, Itse sat on the bed, shaking his head. "Baby, you shouldn't have let them get into your head. We've already discussed this. We've both decided this isn't the right time."

"No, YOU decided!" *Omasan yelled, pointing at him.* "YOU were the one who brainwashed me into thinking we have to continue aspiring to God-knows-what, until we can finally do the right thing and settle down properly."

His eyes hardened as he returned her gaze. "We both agreed that we need to be more settled, you at the practice, and me with a better job than a government hospital that pays peanuts." He waved both hands in exasperation. "For crying out loud, didn't we agree to start the process of relocating to America?

She crossed her arms and shook her head. "I didn't agree to anything, Itse. You're the one who's been trying to shove that relocation agenda down my throat."

He nodded and stood. "But of course, why would the hot shot Pediatrician making seven figures monthly want to relocate to America? Of course, that's a banana just for us low earning monkeys."

She hissed. "Trust you to trivialize everything. The point isn't about who wants to go to America or not, but the fact we've been together almost twenty years, living together for thirteen, but with zero, absolutely zero, plans of making any firm commitment to each other."

He sighed. "Baby, I understand. The pressure from your folks has set you on edge, and I get it. But, we're not ready…"

She stared back at him, her eyes glistening with unshed tears. "I'm thirty-seven years old, Itse. When am I going to be ready?"

They sat in a face off for a while, before she turned around, wiping tears from her face.

"Don't worry about ordering me anything. I'm not hungry."

"Omasan, don't be like this."

She sat on the bed and slipped off her shoes. "No, seriously. I'm good. You should get going. Doesn't the evening shift start at 7? You barely have enough time to make it there."

He hesitated. "Are you sure?"

She waved him off again, not looking at him. "I'm good, Itse. I'll just have a shower and sleep."

"Call me if you need anything, okay?"

She looked up, a brow raised. "Why you dey talk like say na side chick you bring house for the first time?"

He raised his hands again, laughing. "Ah, abeg o! Before my crime becomes one I know nothing about."

"Na so."

He paused by the door, his laughter abated. "Get some sleep, babes. You'll feel much better after a good night's rest."

She smiled and raised her hand in a salute. "Yes, Sir."

Looking at her, his smile waned just as his heart expanded. "I love you."

She nodded and looked away. He waited a few seconds, in expectation, before finally leaving the room. When he was gone, with her hands resting on either side of the bed, she shut her eyes, crestfallen.

THE MARRIAGE CLASS

The next morning, he walked into the house after his shift at the hospital. He kicked off his shoes, set his laptop bag on the dining table, and walked into the kitchen, opening the fridge and scanning it for something to eat. Not finding anything, he grabbed a box of apple juice, took a swig from it, and walked out of the kitchen.

Opening their bedroom door, he stopped in his tracks when he found the room empty, and the bed perfectly made. Frowning, he looked at the clock. It was only 8:30am. Reaching for his phone, he dialed Omasan's number.

The number you have dialed is switched off.

His frown deepened and he dialed another number. This time it connected.

"Hi, Mabel. How are you this morning? Please, is Omasan already at the hospital? She got back from her trip only last night, and I didn't think she was working today." His frown deepened further. "She's not coming in today? Yeah, that's what I thought." He exhaled and rubbed his forehead. "If she does come in by any chance, please ask her to call me. I can't seem to reach her number. Thank you."

The call disconnected, he plopped on the bed, frowning as he wondered what was going on. That was when he saw the note on the bedside table.

We want different things. Don't look for me.

He glared at the note, reading and re-reading it, before letting out a guttural yell as he flung it across the room.

Itse smiles at Omasan, who has now softened enough to return his smile.

"The race isn't always to the swift," he says, still smiling at his fiancée. "It's not how fast, but how well. We always knew we would end up together."

Maxwell's smile is more congenial now, his concerns clearly abated. "Good to know. Congratulations."

Ifeyinwa turns to the last couple, her smile nowhere as enthusiastic as it was at the beginning of the class.

Girl, you and me both!

"Last, and by no means the least, is this couple over here," she says, smiling at the pregnant couple.

The woman returns her smile. "Hi, my name is Nkoyo, and this is Nosa. Until recently, we were colleagues at Hevlos Merchant Bank."

Ifeyinwa beamed at them. "Well, it's nice to meet you, Nkoyo and Nosa. How did you two decide to get married?

I chuckle under my breath, my eyes darting to Nkoyo's extended belly. Isn't it obvious?

The bespectacled Nosa clears his throat. "No story, really. We met, fell in love, and decided."

THE MARRIAGE CLASS

Hevlos Merchant Bank – February 09, 2022

Nosa had a broad smile on his face as he talked on the phone. "Baby, why are you teasing me like this? Or do you want me to beg?" He chuckled. "Yes, I know I left you just this morning. And yes, I know we didn't even get out of bed the whole weekend." He chuckled again. "But after being apart for so long, I think I can be forgiven for wanting to be with you every single moment of every single…"

A knock on his door interrupted him, and a smiling Nkoyo peered into the room.

"Do you have a minute?"

The smile on his face faded. "Let me call you back," he said to the person on the phone.

Nkoyo walked into the office before he could answer her question, still smiling. "Sorry for interrupting your call. Your girlfriend?"

He cleared his throat and nodded. "Yeah."

"Awww, lovely," Nkoyo said, reaching for the picture of a smiling dark-skinned woman on his table. "I see this has returned to your desk as well."

Nosa cleared his throat again. "I decided to bring it back." By now, his impatience had started to show. "Can I help you with anything?"

Her own smile waned as she held his gaze.

Hevlos Merchant Bank – December 20, 2021

Nosa was kissing Nkoyo, backing her into his desk and hoisting her onto it. With one hand, he cleared the contents of his table, sending folders and documents crashing to the floor as he and Nkoyo gave in to their passion.

The next day, Nkoyo couldn't wipe off the smile of bliss and sheer contentment from her face, a dreamy look as she swiveled in her chair, reliving the passionate encounter with Nosa, one of many they'd had since they started hooking up three weeks before. The conference room doors swung open and Nosa and a few other senior executives filed out with some high profile clients. Her heart raced as she stared at him, trying to make eye contact, but he kept his gaze deliberately averted.

Taking a selfie, she smiled as she captioned it, **Missing you already**.

She sent the message to him, and across the hall, she watched him pull his phone out of his pocket, his face still expressionless.

Watching their exchange, the person seated in the workstation next to hers, Liatu, harrumphed. "I hear you and Nosa have been hooking up. Doesn't he have a girlfriend?"

THE MARRIAGE CLASS

Nkoyo turned to her, the look on her face, smug. "Had a girlfriend."

As Nosa walked back to his office, he texted on his phone and Nkoyo's phone soon vibrated with his message.

My place after work?

A wide smile broke on her face as she happily replied; **I'm ready anytime you are.**

Liatu watched, amused. "I thought you were a lot smarter than this. He's obviously on the rebound."

Nkoyo glared at her. "And you know that how?"

Liatu rolled her chair closer. "Jeff and Obinna told me he's been a wreck since he broke up with his babe. Apparently, they were together for years."

Nkoyo hissed and turned her back to Liatu. "If you knew they'd broken up, why were you asking me silly questions? It would do you a lot of good to stop poking your head where it has no business." She started to gather her things and clicked her mouse to shut down her system. "Maybe if you did, you'd free up your time to find yourself someone."

Liatu cackled. "I'd rather be single than anyone's sloppy seconds. Not at my age, and definitely not at yours!"

Ignoring her, Nkoyo's eyes were on Nosa as he emerged from his office. With the most indecipherable of nods, he walked out. Picking up her bag, she rushed after him.

ADESUWA O'MAN NWOKEDI

Nosa's Car - January 18, 2022

Nosa and Nkoyo were sitting in silence, the only sound coming from the purr of the car engine. She looked desolate and he, penitent.

"If you knew you'd go back to her, why did you string me along like that?"

"I didn't string you along, Nkoyo," he sighed. "And I'm sorry if it came across that way. If I knew you were reading so much meaning into it, I wouldn't have let it go on for as long as it did. I thought, like me, you only wanted something casual."

A tear rolled down her face, and she made no attempt to stop it.

"So, you're really going back to her?"

He sighed again and was quiet for a while. "I love her, Nkoyo."

Nkoyo nodded in sad acceptance. Without another word, she opened the car and walked out.

He made to call after her, to say anything to appease her, but changed his mind. Instead, he sighed, started the car, and drove off.

Havlos Merchant Bank - February 09, 2022

Nosa cleared his throat again. "Can I help you with anything?"

Nkoyo said nothing as her eyes held his for a while.

THE MARRIAGE CLASS

"Can we talk later?" he asked, rising to his feet. "I really have to leave the office now."

"I'm pregnant."

His eyes widened and he stared at her, frozen to the spot.

"You're...you're..."

She squared her shoulders, her eyes boldly holding his. "Pregnant, Nosa. Pregnant with your child."

His legs gave way, and he dropped in a heap in his chair, his eyes as wide as if he had seen a ghost.

Nosa shrugs. "So, yeah. We met, fell in love and, well, here we are."

Ifeyinwa nods and smiles. "That's lovely. Congratulations. For everything."

Maxwell lets out an exaggerated sigh. "Wow! What an evening this has been! You see why this introductory class is my favorite?" Grinning, he looks at his wife. "I proposed to this beautiful woman here one hot Sunday afternoon in December 1995, as we sat in a long queue at the petrol station waiting to buy fuel. Sitting in my Nissan Bluebird, roasting in the heat because the car, being tenth-hand, had no air conditioning, I looked at the beautiful woman sitting next to me, a beautiful woman that could have been anywhere else, with anyone else, instead of sweating buckets in a fuel queue, and I knew I had to marry her. So, in that hot car, I asked her. And she said yes."

"The best decision of my life," Ifeyinwa says, smiling at her husband, before turning back to the class. "One of the reasons we do this, why we ask to hear about each couple, is to show you how different we all are. Apart from being different as individuals, our circumstances are different, our love stories are different, our relationships are different. You can see how, with ten couples here, no two stories are the same. And that's what makes us special. It's what makes this beautiful thing that has brought us to this class special." She straightens and smiles. "And my husband and I are pleased and honoured to help guide you as you prepare to take the most important journey of your life."

As we file out of the class, I panic when I see that it is almost 10pm. Walking to my car, I don't even bother to keep in step with Raymond.

"Abi! Abi, wait up!" he calls out.

I ignore him and continue to walk to my car, a big scowl on my face.

"Are you upset about having to drive back so late at night?" he chuckles, when he catches up with me. "I did offer to pick you up."

I turn around to face him. "Do you really expect me to make this drive every week? Do you really expect me to drive to the mainland every week for this class?"

THE MARRIAGE CLASS

Raymond laughs. "It's actually two times a week."

I let out a long hiss, but he holds my hand as I reach to open my car.

"Sweetness, you don't have to drive. I told you it would be my pleasure to pick you up. Trust me, I'm not happy either about you driving home at this time." He sighed and looked around. "Listen, I'll pay a guard to watch your car overnight. Let me take you home, and I'll have someone pick up your car tomorrow."

I look at him, and rather than be touched by his concern, I am infuriated by it.

"How can you stand there, acting all nice and loving, after I called you another man's name in there?"

He looks at me, momentarily confused, before shrugging. "It was a mistake. I know you didn't mean to call me that."

"What kind of mistake?" I yell in exasperation, hitting his chest with my fists. "I called you another man's name in our marriage class, but rather than get mad, you're making excuses for me?"

Raymond holds my hands with his. "Sweetness, relax, okay? You're wound up about having to come all this way. I get it."

I shove him and step back, shaking my head. "My God! Why are you this passive, Raymond? Why?"

The smile fades from his face and his gaze becomes more serious. "What would you rather I do, Abi? Throw a fit every time you call me his name or stalk him on IG?"

I deflate, surprised he is aware that I have, indeed, been stalking Lucas, even if Instagram is only one of the many platforms that this prowling has taken place. Awash with guilt, I place my hands on his chest and he pulls me in for a hug.

"Let me drive you home, baby," he whispers in my ear in our embrace. "We could both do with a glass of wine…and whatever else comes after that."

I smile as I pull back, his soft gaze making my heart melt. Raymond is the only man I've ever been with that has never left me guessing. He wears his love for me on his sleeve, and being with him is like sailing in tranquil, calm waters - beautiful and stress-free.

Except I now find myself missing…wanting…turbulence.

"I better go," I say, patting his face. "I'll call you when I get home."

He nods and kisses my forehead. "Drive safe. No road rage, please."

"It's the middle of the night and the roads are empty," I grin as I let myself into my car. "Lucky for everyone." Blowing him a kiss, I shut the door.

He taps on the window, making me slide it down.

THE MARRIAGE CLASS

"The next class is on Friday. I'd really prefer to pick you up, so you don't have to drive home so late."

I sigh and shrug, too tired to argue. "Okay."

As I put my Honda CR-V in reverse, as I wave goodbye, all I can do is wonder why the thought of returning for another class is giving me the same reaction I had when I was ill as a kid, and forced to drink cups of herbal tea that tasted like piss.

And why I am comparing our wedding to a vile, sour liquid.

Ewa & Sanya

Ewa is standing by Sanya's car, and shakes her head as the Honda CR-V pulls out of the park.

"Na wa o!" she remarks.

Sanya bades goodbye to the men he is talking to, Itse and Boma, and walks up to his car.

"'Na wa' what?" he asks, getting into his BMW X6.

"That guy, I feel so sorry for him," Ewa answers, pointing where Raymond is still standing, waving at the departing car. "First of all, he waited almost an hour before his fiancée arrived. Then she called him another man's name, did you notice?"

Sanya sighs and shakes his head as he starts the car. "No, I didn't notice anything."

Ewa claps her hands and shakes her head again, spoiling for a good gossip. "Something about them just seems off. Why would they come for their marriage class in separate cars anyway?"

Sanya turns to her. "Ewatomi, mind your business. All couples have issues and theirs have nothing to do with us."

Hissing, she crosses her arms and turns away, just as their car pulls out of the premises.

Omasan & Itse

Itse is laughing to a joke Boma has cracked, and his eyes drift where Omasan and April are standing. His laughter fades when he recognizes the bored look on his fiancée's face.

"I better go. It was nice meeting you, man."

Boma shakes his hand enthusiastically. "Ditto, my brother." He chuckles. "I love your sense of humour."

Itse smiles and takes a deep breath as he and Boma approach the women. "If only everyone liked it as much," he mutters to himself.

Seeing him approach, Omasan turns to April. "It was nice meeting you. See you on Friday."

April beams, her eyes twinkling. "See you on Friday." She grins at Itse. "You two make such a lovely couple. I hope Boma and I are still like this after nineteen years. You two don't look your age at all."

Boma winces. He turns to Omasan, embarrassed. "What she meant to say was…"

Omasan smiles at him. "It's okay. Take care."

Itse's smile is stiff, just as Omasan brushes past him to their waiting car.

"Nice meeting you, April. See you later, Boma."

He turns around and walks to the car, opens the door and gets inside. Omasan immediately turns to glower at him.

"What was all that about me giving you an ultimatum? Why did you have to humiliate me like that?"

Itse rolls his eyes. "I never said anything about you giving me an ultimatum. I only laughed when the other guy said he got one."

"You laughed in agreement, like you could empathize."

Itse turns to her, his wide eyes registering his frustration and increasing annoyance. "Well, maybe I can."

She glares back at him. "Nobody gave you an ultimatum. You didn't have to come after me. When I moved out, I released you to do whatever it was you wanted to. You're the one who came to beg me to come back."

He sighs and starts the car. "It's been a long day, *abeg*. Let's just go."

With both their faces tight, their car pulls out of the car park.

Ivie & Eric

A chauffeur-driven Audi pulls up in front of Eric and Ivie. She turns to look at him, confused.

"Your other car is here? I thought we were going home together."

Eric shakes his head. "Don't you want some space after all of that? I know I do."

She smiles, even though the hurt is evident on her face. "You talk like being with me is some kind of punishment."

He groans, just as another chauffeur-driven car, a Mercedes, pulls up in front of them.

"Ivie, for the love of God! You can come back to my place tomorrow. I just need a break tonight. Please!"

She nods in acquiescence, not saying anything. He sighs and kisses her on the cheek.

"I'll call you when I get home. We'll do lunch tomorrow, okay?" He winks at her. "And dinner. And breakfast the morning after."

She smiles at him, appeased. "And I know you'll make it worth my while."

He winks at her again, as he gets into the Mercedes. "You got that right, kid."

"I love you," she says.

"Ciao!" he answers, blowing her a kiss.

She watches as the car drives off, just as the rumble of thunder rips through the night air. In the far distance, Bianca looks up at the sky in dismay.

"It looks like it's going to rain. Do you need a ride?" Ivie calls out.

Bianca stares at her, wide-eyed, surprised by the offer and also in awe of the flashy car parked in front of them.

"I wouldn't want to take you out of your way. I'm headed to Surulere."

The smile on Ivie's face widens as she opens the car door, making a quick mental change of plans. If Eric doesn't want to be with her tonight, she's sure her parents will. "I'm headed to Aguda, so you're in luck."

With a wide smile, Bianca gets into the car.

Nkoyo & Nosa

Nkoyo and Nosa are walking to his car. He is holding her with one hand, and her handbag with the other.

"That was so long and tedious!" she hisses and shakes her head. "And to think this was just the introductory class. What will the others now be like?"

Nosa turns to her, concern on his face. "Would you like us to check out the church near your estate, to see if we can join their class instead?"

She shakes her head and sighs.

"I already checked, or have you forgotten? Their class is six months long. We don't have six months."

He nods as they approach the car, opens the door, and helps her into it.

"I need something sweet to calm my nerves," she calls out as he walks over to the driver's side. "Let's get some ice-cream on the way home."

He nods as he lets himself into the car. Once seated, he involuntarily exhales.

She turns to look at him. "Is everything okay?"

He turns and offers her a strained smile. "Everything's fine. And ice-cream sounds like a fantastic idea."

With that, he kicks the car into motion and drives off.

Chioma & A.K.

A.K. and Chioma exchange a glance after overhearing Nkoyo's demand, before they burst into laughter.

"And what about you, my love? Do you also need 'something sweet to calm your nerves'?" A.K. sniggers.

"That woman looks the kind of person who will milk the life out of her pregnancy. She has that guy on a short leash," Chioma giggles.

"Not that I blame him, though. When you're pregnant, there's nothing you won't be able to get me to do."

With the smile still on her face, she winks at him. "Well then, we better hurry up and get married so you can show me, rather than simply tell."

He bends his face so close to hers, they are less than an inch apart.

"How about we go back home and start practicing?"

She blushes before dissolving into more giggles as he kisses her on the bridge of her nose.

Ogechi & Zulu

Ogechi and Zulu are walking to his car. She is watching A.K. and Chioma as they flirt, a wistful look on her face.

"Oge," Zulu calls her name.

She turns to him, realizing she missed what he said.

"Huh?"

"I was asking if you're feeling okay. You haven't said much since we left the class."

She shrugs. "I'm just tired. It was rather tedious hearing from so many couples."

THE MARRIAGE CLASS

He laughs, putting his arm around her shoulder, inadvertently roughing her blouse. She frowns, irritated.

"Take it easy," she mutters, adjusting herself to release the part of her Givenchy blouse his hold has caught.

"I enjoyed it. I liked hearing so many stories," he says, oblivious of her irritation. Shaking his head, he chuckles again. "Last, last, our own is still better than many others."

She glares at him. "Seriously? That was your takeaway from the whole thing."

He clucks his mouth, his laughter disappearing. "*Biko*, I don't have energy for your stress this evening. Can't anyone joke with you?"

They approach his car and she gets into it, ignoring him. He stands there, glaring at the vehicle for a few moments, before walking over to the driver's side.

"And I don't know what kind of spirit made you convince me to drive all this way myself tonight," he mutters as he gets in.

Kris & Bola

Seated in Bola's car, Kris straps on her seat belt and smiles at him.

"That was actually not a bad experience. I think I'm going to quite like this class."

Bola nods in agreement. "I like the counselors. They seem really nice and easy going."

Kris nods as well. "Very. And there were no ageist remarks either."

Bola shakes his head and chuckles. "Babes, you look younger and more beautiful than all the women in that class."

She smiles at him and strokes his face. "You're such a liar, but I love you regardless."

He laughs and she leans in for a kiss. Pulling back, she smiles at him.

"So…we're really doing this?"

He smiles at her and nods. "We're really doing this, my dear wife-to-be. So, sit back, relax, and enjoy the ride."

She smiles with him, as he starts the ignition and drives out of the car park.

2. THE REBOUND

Beliefs & Expectations

"Today's topic is all about beliefs and expectations," Ifeyinwa says, as she begins our next class, her eyes moving from one couple to the next. "And how realistic the ones we have, and make, are, especially when it comes to our partners."

As she talks, Raymond's hand brushes mine as he writes, and we exchange a smile. He returns his attention to Ifeyinwa, and I can't help but think how wide and diverse our individual belief systems truly can be, the absurdity of trying to align these systems of two very different people. Over a year into our relationship, and it still takes me aback when I wake up in Raymond's house to see he has ironed my clothes, run me a bath, and made me breakfast. Even when we're not together, I am still overwhelmed when he sends me food at work - breakfast trays, takeaway from my favourite Chinese restaurant, or *jollof* rice from Ghana High. Growing up, it was the norm for my mother to wait on my father hand and foot, so having someone do that to me, wait on me and consistently put my needs above his own, as heart melting as it is, is alien…and a tad smothering.

April & Boma

Boma's mind wanders as Ifeyinwa talks, unable to focus on what the marriage counselor is saying. Next to him, April is nodding enthusiastically as she takes notes. Glancing at her notepad, he can see words like *perspective, commitment,* and *compromise*. And he wonders if he's ready to do any.

Especially the compromise. The never ending compromise.

"Why do people expect a story about my name?" she had asked on their way home on Monday. "Is everyone expected to explain the origin of their name?"

"It's not a common name, April. People would probably also expect a story from someone called May or June."

She'd shrugged and whipped out her phone, scrolling through her social media feed, as she was wont to do when their conversations got uncomfortable.

"Baby, about Itse and Omasan, the couple we were just with," he'd said, glancing at her. "I don't think it's a good idea to reference their age like that. They might already be sensitive about doing this after so long and might not like any reminders about it."

"What did I say? I told them they don't look their age? Is that an insult?" April had demanded, turning to glare at him.

"Hey, baby, no need to bite my head," he'd said, laughing to defuse the rising tension in the car. "No need to practice what you've learned in your Taekwondo class on me."

"It's kickboxing, not Taekwondo," she'd answered, returning her attention to her phone. "Anyway, can we pass by Ocean View? Do you think they'll still be open? I'm desperate for a burger."

"Ocean View, huh? Why view the ocean, when we could simply wave at it?" he'd chuckled, glancing at her.

She'd frowned and shook her head. "Wave at it?"

The smile on his face faded as he returned his attention to the road, not ready to break down the joke the way he did for every other joke he told. "Never mind."

Shrugging, she'd continued scrolling through her phone, giggling as she watched a cross dresser's skit on Instagram. Boma glanced at her as she laughed, and wondered if that was what life would be like for them…for him…forever.

Because forever was a very long time.

He had always thought himself a sapiosexual, attracted to a woman's intelligence before he even noticed anything about her physical appearance. Never one to take himself seriously, people had always been drawn to him because of his quick wit and humour. Nothing turned him on more than a woman able to spar with him, and Felicity, his ex-girlfriend, had been able to do just that. There was never a dull moment with her, and she could engage anyone on everything from politics, to sports, to pop culture, to the cheesy jokes that were his leaning. Whenever they were together, they sparred non-stop, tossing jokes and sound bites back and forth like they were playing a game of Ping-Pong. She'd been his dream girl, his intellectual equal, and for six years, had made him the happiest he'd ever been. Until she'd left him for a Europe-based doctor she met in her village that Christmas of 2020.

Crushed and heartbroken, Boma spent all of 2021 making his way through women like a tornado collecting debris. Determined never to give his heart away again, he'd picked up women for one thing, and one thing only; sex. He was no longer interested in anything else, no longer keen on letting anyone in.

Until he met April.

On New Year's Day, after deciding not to go, he'd made the last minute decision to attend a friend's birthday party. There, he'd been introduced to a girl with the brownest eyes and deepest dimples he had ever seen. As she talked and gesticulated about God-knew-what, he'd been transfixed by the way the dimples burrowed her cheeks, and the tingle-tingle sound of her laughter. She had an innocent, child-like charm that drew him in the longer they spoke. They ended up in bed that night, and her sexual prowess belied her innocent charm. There was nothing innocent about the way she had kissed, swilled, lapped, and straddled him, doing things to him that made all the sex he'd had with any other woman, Felicity included, seem like a poor substitute, a dry run for the real thing - emphasis on the word *dry*. And he'd decided, there and then, never to let this one go, proposing to her only two months later.

But now, in the fifth month of their relationship and three months to their wedding, the sex, even though still out-of-this world amazing, is no longer enough.

"You're not writing," April peers at his blank notepad, a notepad that had been his idea for them to bring. "This is a very important topic, so you need to listen."

Boma turns to her and smiles. "I'm listening."

It is a bold faced lie. He hasn't heard a word after Ifeyinwa's opener. Picking up his pen, he focuses on their instructor, scribbling the last part of whatever list it is she is reeling off, underlining the last phrase about managing expectations. Maybe that's what he needs to do – manage his expectations. Maybe it is unfair to expect April to be everything Felicity was – funny, smart, intellectual – as well as everything she wasn't – a powerhouse in bed.

"That was a really great class," April says, as they walk into his apartment later that night. Thankfully, the class didn't exceed its designed one-hour duration, so they are home before 9pm.

"Yeah, it was," he says, throwing his car key on the dining table and walking to the living room.

"Oh, that reminds me," she says, sitting on the sofa. "I found this affordable package for a honeymoon in Dubai. It comes with a safari and even a trip to Abu Dhabi."

"Sounds good," he says, sitting next to her, grinning. "Do you know the difference between Dubai and Abu Dhabi?"

"What?" she asks, certain she does not.

"While people in Dubai don't like the Flintstones, people in Abu Dhabi Dooo!"

She stares at him, her face expressionless, causing the smile on his to disappear.

"Anyway," she says, steering the conversation in the direction it needs to be, which is far away from his strange jokes. "The caterers have gotten back to my mom, Havana Meals says they'll charge five million, while Gold Lily says they'll charge about five hundred grand less."

Boma's brows knot and he turns to her. "That's steep. Do they know it's only for two hundred guests?"

April giggles and she swings her feet across his thighs. "You and this 'two hundred guests' business. I already told you my parents say five hundred is a more realistic number."

THE MARRIAGE CLASS

The knot between his brows deepens. "Even at five hundred guests, that's still about ten thousand naira per person."

She shrugs and picks up the remote control.

"Is that how much they are charging?" he presses. "Ten thousand naira per person?"

"How am I supposed to know that, Boma?" she mutters. "We told them what we want – continental, local, some grills for later – and that's the quote they sent."

"But you need to know the breakdown, to be able to…" he begins, but sees he has already lost her attention to a rerun of *Keeping Up with the Kardashians* on the E! channel.

As she laughs at the screen, he is awash with a cold wave, the reality that this is what life is going to be for them…for him. Her disinterest in the finer details is not peculiar to the caterers' quotes, but all the costs related to their wedding. She has refused to use the spreadsheet he prepared, has no idea by how much they have exceeded their ten-million-naira budget - because he knows they have exceeded it - and has not even asked how the ten-million-naira spend will affect his business expansion plans.

"And that doesn't include small chops and desserts," she says, turning to him, the need to iterate that fact greater than her need to see Kim and Kourtney rant about their sister's cheating baby daddy. "Those are different vendors.

We probably need to budget about two to three million for those."

"That's almost the entire wedding budget, April," he reminds her. "We need to find a way to shave these food-related costs by at least half."

"Stop playing, Boma," she says, turning back to the TV, giggling like he has cracked some joke he's not aware of. If only his real jokes made her laugh like that. "Shave what? Don't let me smack you with this throw pillow."

"And give me a con-cushion?" he chuckles.

She turns to him, her laughter gone, her nose wrinkled, and her head cocked to the side.

Another joke right over her head.

"Why are you acting like you don't have money? What about the money you've got in your dollar account?" she asks. "With the current exchange rate, we can get a lot to add to the wedding budget."

"That's money for my store expansion plans, April," Boma answers, an edge now in his voice. "I've been saving that for over four years and it's not money I can touch. You know this."

She shrugs and returns her attention to the TV, raising the remote control to change the channel. "I guess you'll just have to take a loan then, because this wedding is definitely going to cost more than ten million. Have you forgotten the venue alone is costing us three million? And we haven't even talked about the traditional wedding. I told you my dad says we can't have it in our house, right? Then, my dresses, the one for the ceremony and the one for the reception…"

He watches her talk, seeing her lips move but not hearing a word, the disinterest she has shown in the thing, the one thing he has been chasing and aspiring towards for years, a hard slap across his face.

Beliefs and expectations.

Is it too much to believe in the kind of compatibility where your partner feels your pinch points and struggles the same way you do? Is it too much to expect to have a reasonable conversation with the person you intend to spend the rest of your life with, without feeling frustrated, exasperated, or just plain disappointed?

Painfully aware that Boma is not listening to her, April is unable to stop talking, reeling off all the things they need for their wedding, many of which she has told him before. Her heart plummets when he finally looks away, and her brain scrambles for something, anything, to say. She knows that look on his face, the look he has when she is unable to understand his weird jokes, but there is something about tonight that seems different.

She fell for him immediately they met, the light-skinned guy with the big afro, and wide eyes that looked at her like she was the sun, moon, and all the planets in the galaxy rolled into one. When he asked her to marry him only weeks later, she'd happily jumped at the opportunity, and not just because she was desperate to be married before her thirtieth birthday. But now, as he pours himself a glass of water, she can't remember when last he looked at her like that...like she was the sun, moon, and all the planets in the galaxy rolled into one.

"This wedding is costing a fortune," he says, a smile forming on his face as he shakes his head. "Like Dracula." He looks at her, the smile fading. "You know, a pain in the neck."

She doesn't understand the correlation but pretends she does, releasing a sound she hopes sounds like laughter, patting the arm of the chair as she does. His smile is completely gone now, a brow raised as he looks at her, and she knows he can tell she's faking the laughter...and didn't understand the joke at all.

Beliefs and expectations.

Is it too much to believe a man that smart and driven will want her? Is it too much to expect him not to place the heavy weight of his expectations on her? For his every look, his every word not to convey just how far she is from meeting these? Is too much to be loved and accepted for the person she is?

And not a clone of his former lover?

3. SOCIAL NOT-WORKING

Money

Ewa & Sanya

Standing in front of a full-length mirror, Ewa runs her hands through the thick honey-blond tresses of her body-wave wig, tilting her head left to right to be sure she looks good from every angle, especially after the highlighter and bronzer disaster she had with her last Instagram post. Nah, her brand can not afford another faux pas like that.

"The lips need more gloss," she says to the woman standing less than a foot away watching her with an impassive face, the rap of fingers on the table on which her entire cosmetics portmanteau lies upturned the giveaway of her rising impatience. When there is no response, Ewa looks up, meeting the woman's eyes in the mirror. "Rike, did you hear me?"

"Any more gloss and the hair will stick to your lips when you start taking pictures," Rike answers, the even tone of her voice a struggle. "Remember what happened last time." She glances at her wristwatch. "Is this going to take much longer?" It is past 4pm and she has been there since before 10 in the morning.

"A few more minutes," Ewa answers, primping her hair again and stepping away from the mirror, aware she has said that to Rike at least six times in the last hour. Turning to Kayla, her stylist, she smiles. "You were right about this corset belt. It's given the outfit more *oomph*!"

Kayla gives Ewa a thumbs up from where she stands by Alaba, the eager undergraduate Ewa hired as a Personal Assistant after she spammed Ewa's DM with several messages 'stanning' her. Alaba is stationed by two sixteen-inch ring lights hoisting two phones, one an iPhone and the other a Samsung, both of them top of the range, both of them not yet paid for. As a matter of fact, in that room, the ring lights are the only things that have been paid for…in part.

"Okay, let's do this!" Ewa says, projecting her voice, raising her hands and snapping her fingers the way she does before every shoot, to get herself gingered to create the kind of content that has gained for her almost a million followers on Instagram. "Play me my song!"

THE MARRIAGE CLASS

As Toby Shang's *Run This Town* plays, she positions herself in the spot of the living room she most favours for shots, a stark white wall with a large Yucca Plant that stands almost six feet tall.

"Let's start with the close-up shots while the makeup is still fresh," she says, standing with her legs apart and her hands positioned on her slender hips angled to give the impression of width, the red silk jumpsuit she wears cinched by a wide, white corset belt so tight, her inflow and outflow of air is constricted, the two streams clashing in her airway. For these shots, these shots she knows will be *fire* on the 'gram, she can endure a little bit of pain.

"Yasss, queen!" Alaba says, clicking away with Ewa's most recent purchase, a Nikon Z 50 camera, the phones on the ring holders programmed for videos only, as Ewa stands a few degrees slanted from the camera, her face in a glower, like the pictures are an inconvenience. "These shots are gi-vi-ng!"

Rike and Kayla stand, waiting as Alaba takes the pictures - the scowling poses, the cross-armed boss bitch poses, and the shut-eyed, wide-smiled, life-is-beautiful poses. It goes on forever. Not even Kayla's audible exaggerated sighs are enough to punctuate the marathon photo session. In truth, what exasperates them, Rike and Kayla, is not the lengthy shoot – they have had many of such with Ewa – but the fact they haven't been paid for the last few; Rike for over four and Kayla for a good six.

"Awesome! These are amazing!" Ewa says, beaming as she scrolls through the images Alaba sends to her phone over an hour later. "You're awesome."

"Thanks," Alaba answers, before clearing her throat. "Ewa, you said to remind you about my salary…"

"Yeah, I'm on it," Ewa says, not taking her eyes off her phone as she uploads the pictures to her Instagram page after running them through a filter she has an expensive subscription for, captioning them #OOTD, #ScarletQueen, #BossBitchesWearRed.

From the corner of her eye, Ewa can see Rike and Kayla still hanging around, and she scans her head for where to quickly get some money to pay them, because, if their body language is anything to go by, it is unlikely they will show up again if they aren't paid today. Her phone starts to vibrate, and she squints at the unknown number, contemplating whether to answer it. As she is still hoping to hear from some of the brands she has advertised for on occasion, she decides to, lest she miss out on much needed business.

Big mistake.

"Ewatomi, so it's gotten to the point I have to call you with another number?" a voice screams from the other end of the line. "Is it until I drag you online before you pay me? It's been almost a month and I'm losing my patience!"

Ewa rubs her forehead and steps away from the group around her, as if they can somehow hear the irate person

THE MARRIAGE CLASS

on the phone. "Doyin, I swear I'll pay you this week. The money I've been waiting for…"

"Fuck all these excuses! I'm tired of your lies!" Doyin cuts in. "Listen, I'm giving you until tomorrow, or else you'll see what I'll do to you online. *Oni gbese!*"

Ewa grits her teeth as her nostrils flare, the insult hitting its mark. "You'll get your money."

As soon as the line disconnects, Ewa blocks the number, just as she thinks about what excuse she will give Sanya for why she needs another million naira bail out, less than two weeks after the last one.

And speaking of Sanya.

Let into the apartment by Mama Ayo, Ewa's aunt's housekeeper, Sanya frowns as he walks into the living room just as Kayla is wheeling out racks of clothes, her other hand burdened with a large bag containing accessories. Rike is arranging her makeup in the various compartments of a large bag and Alaba is disassembling the ring lights. Sanya purses his lips, the Tony Shang song playing on repeat letting him know there has been yet another elaborate photo shoot there.

"Hey, baby," Ewa blows him a kiss, her eyes briefly flitting to him before returning to her phone as she resumes captioning her pictures, needing every hashtag that will beat Instagram's algorithm and make her posts more visible. "Don't worry, I'll soon change. We won't be late for class, I promise."

"Were you filming a sponsored post?" Sanya asks.

She shakes her head, still focused on her captioning. "No, just content for my page."

"And that's why you got all these people here?" he asks, his voice several decibels higher than it typically is, causing Ewa to finally look up, a frown setting on her face.

"This is my glam squad, Sanya. Why are you acting like you haven't seen them before? And Alaba is my Personal Assistant, in case you've forgotten."

Alaba and Rike exchange a glance, before they both hasten out of the room.

"I hope you're happy now," Ewa says, her eyes narrow and her captioning forgotten. "I hope you're happy humiliating me in front of my squad."

"What dirty squad?" Sanya exclaims, his exasperation rising. "For an Instagram picture you could have taken yourself? How much did this shoot cost, Ewa? I know Rike doesn't come cheap, and this is the third time I've seen her here in…"

"Why are you talking like an illiterate, Sanya?" she cuts in. "Why are you talking like you don't understand why I must consistently create good content, if I want to attract brands? You, of all people, should know this."

He shakes his head, realizing this is one argument he isn't going to win. "Let's just go, Ewa. It's almost 6pm."

THE MARRIAGE CLASS

Hissing, she sweeps past him in the direction of her bedroom, returning ten minutes later in another jumpsuit, this time in *adire*, the scarlet red lipstick replaced by a matte wine. Beautiful though she looks, Sanya isn't moved to pay her any compliments, and they make the trip to St. Claire's in angry silence.

"Today's class is about money," Maxwell says, introducing the class with a grin. "What do they say about it being the root of all evil? Well, there just might be some truth to that, as money is one of the top five reasons couples divorce. And, with every generation - from Boomers, to Gen Xers, to Millennials - the percentage of couples that divorce as a result of money problems rises exponentially. In a survey conducted last year, twenty-nine percent of Boomers said they ended their marriage due to disagreements about money, and this number rose to forty-one percent for Gen Xers." He shrugs and chuckles. "Can you imagine what that number will be like for Gen Z couples?"

Even though it is an interesting topic, my phone has stolen my attention more than anything, the lure to read new congratulatory messages on Lucas's post stronger than my desire to learn how to cope with my partner's different approach to finances. Swiping up my screen, Lucas's smiling profile picture greets me as the LinkedIn app opens. I turn to Raymond and our eyes hold. I smile at him, turning my phone face down, praying with everything inside me that he didn't see what I was doing…or the face of the man whose picture I have looked at so many times in the last week, it is now etched into my memory. Raymond returns my smile and places his hand over mine, making me heave a sigh of relief, grateful he didn't catch me ogling the man - the one man - I shouldn't.

"I got you something," Raymond says during a short break, handing me a small gift box. "To make up for dragging you all the way to Yaba twice a week."

"Oh, Raymond!" I exclaim, opening the box and beholding the delicate white gold necklace with a sparkling sapphire embedded in a pearl encrusted heart. "This is beautiful! Thank you!"

As I lean over to plant a kiss on his bearded cheek, I wonder why money is touted as such a villain in relationships.

When it can solve a whole multitude of wrongs.

Ewa & Sanya

"That was a great class. Did you notice how everyone was more attentive today?" Sanya attempts conversation as they drive back to the island after the class. "The subject of money is one everyone is interested in."

THE MARRIAGE CLASS

Ewa grunts, her attention on her phone as she scrolls, the frown that has been on her face all evening, tightening. No, he doesn't get to pretend everything is fine after what he did.

He sighs and casts her a sideward glance, sensing she is in the mood for yet another round of marathon malice. While she is an expert in the art, the mere thought of clipped conversations and long faces is enough to make him break into a cold sweat. So, he caves.

"I'm sorry, baby."

She hisses. "Why would you yell at me in front of my staff? Do you know embarrassed I was?"

Your staff or your 'glam squad', which is it? He bites back this retort, knowing no good can come from voicing it, and raises her hand to his lips instead. "I'm sorry, baby."

"Because how else will I get brands interested if I don't create good content?"

He sighs and purses his lips, restraining himself from schooling her on the very many cheaper and more efficient ways she could do just that. Instead, he says again. "I'm sorry, baby."

Appeased, she looks at him, a slow smile curving her lips as her hand rests high on his thigh. "Let's go home."

Home is his bachelor pad, a terrace house in Osborne Estate, Ikoyi, that now houses more of her belongings – clothes, shoes, what looks to him like a million bottles, tubes, and pallets of cosmetics and brushes in every size known to man, and kitchen appliances she is yet to even unbox – than his. As her hand moves higher up his thigh in silent promise of what lies in store for him that night, he is more than happy to oblige. He opens his mouth to tell her, yet again, how much he cannot wait for her to live there permanently, but pauses when he notices her terminate an incoming call.

Ewa glares at her screen as it lights up again with another call, cursing Queenie under her breath for the persistent harassment despite the luxury goods retailer turning down her proposition to pay in installments for the Christian Louboutin, Jimmy Choo, and Amina Muaddi shoes she took possession of months before, shoes she'd estimated to cost a little under a million naira at the time, but which, with the current exchange rate, now have a face value north of two million naira.

"What were you saying, baby?" Ewa says to Sanya, her eyes on her phone as she blocks Queenie's number.

"Just that I can't wait for when you get to be with me forever," he still goes on to say, as he tries to convince himself that whomever she is blocking is probably a troll, leech, or some other kind of nuisance.

Even though, deep inside, he knows it is very likely someone she owes money.

THE MARRIAGE CLASS

As is normal, he feels her stir in the early hours of morning, but unlike when he would normally roll over to the other side as she got out of bed that early, this time, he throws an arm over her, determined to snuggle for longer for a change.

Ewa's eyes widen as Sanya's arm across her chest detains her in the bed. They flit to his sleeping form and she tries to lift his arm, slowly and gently, so as not to rouse him, desperate to run to the bathroom to tidy herself before he awakes.

"Why are you up so early?" his voice is raspy as he pulls her closer. "Lie with me."

Lie with him *ke*? Her eyes fall on her wig lying ungainly on the sofa across the room where she threw it in the middle of the night after he fell asleep, wanting to kick herself for taking it for granted she would retrieve it before he awoke. With the rough cornrows on her head, not to mention the dark Panda circles under her eyes, she cannot afford to 'lie with him'.

"I need to use the toilet," she answers, her hands pawing the table by her bedside, in search of the lamp that is still on, because, with Sanya in that precarious halfway point between being asleep and alert, illumination will not be her friend.

He opens his eyes and before he can say another word, the room is thrown into darkness. But before she can squeeze out from under his hold, he leans over and turns the light back on, and is stunned when she dives under the thick duvet. He tries to pull the duvet back, but her hands clutch its seam, holding to it for dear life. A bubble of rage effervesces from deep inside him and he tugs at it with equal strength, soon overpowering her and peeling it away, revealing her quivering and staring back at him with wide, darting eyes, the look on her face like a sheep's being led to slaughter. With her hair woven into about a dozen plaits, her eyes more visible without its usual long layering of false eyelashes, and her lips a natural blend of brown and pink, his anger evaporates, the warmth in his chest less from rage and more from his heart melting anew at the very sight of her in her most natural state.

"Why are you hiding, Ewa?"

She lets out a long hiss, sits up, swings her feet off the bed, walks to the sofa, picks up what Sanya can now see is her wig, and walks into the bathroom, locking the door firmly behind her.

By this time, all traces of sleep have left his eyes and he sits up in bed - in surprise, in irritation, in disbelief. It is a good thirty-five minutes before the bathroom door opens, and his disgust is amplified when he sees that she has not only showered, but that the wig is back to crowning her head, the false lashes are back on her eyes, her face is matte and flawless in the shade of brown that comes from her liquid foundation, and her lips are a glossy peach. For crying out loud, it's not even 6am.

"Is that why you're up before the crack of dawn every time you're here? Is it too much for you to just lie in bed with me without thinking about all that?" He gestures at the space around her. "Must you always wear that mask with me?"

"This has nothing to do with you," she answers, even though it is only partly true. "I'm an influencer and can't afford to be caught looking anything but ready." In truth, there are a few days when she lies in bed till noon and enjoys the freedom and weightlessness of not having to wear any of the bulky tresses of hair that are the wigs in her large collection, but those are only the days when she has no morning appointments, days when she is able to firmly secure her bedroom door with heavy bolts, barring anyone from entry.

Sanya rises from the bed and walks to her, a smile playing on his face. Getting to her, he wraps his hands around her waist and pulls her to himself, lowering his lips to hers in a kiss, licking off her glossy, but surprisingly tasteless, lipstick. He makes to remove her wig but her hands fly to her head, securing it in place.

"You don't need all this, babe," he says, his eyes holding hers. "Especially these lashes."

She lowers her eyes, self-conscious, hating that she has racked up too high a bill with Saidat, her lash installer, and has not been able to show her face there, hence why she has had to make do with cheaper disposable lashes, instead of the semi-permanent ones that are her usual.

"You're so much more beautiful without all of it."

"Indeed!" she scoffs. "Like you would have slid into my DM if I was some boring looking babe."

He furrows his brows. "Actually, you were the one who slid into *my* DM. Or have you forgotten?"

She looks up at him and rolls her eyes. "I commented on your story. There's a difference."

"No, actually. There's no difference at all," he says, chuckling.

And, indeed, that was how they met. Sanya Wellington gained popularity as a student in the United Kingdom in the early 2000s, modeling in print and on the runway for major luxury brands like Burberry, Prada, and Armani. By the time he quit modeling and moved back to Nigeria at the age of twenty-six after wrapping up his MBA and became a serial entrepreneur investing in startups, stocks, bonds, and digital currencies, he had built a large social media following of his own. A lover of the good life, he loved the opportunity to show it off too, posting pictures from his business and social traipses around the world - pictures of him sitting cross-legged and sipping champagne while flying first class, looking out of balconies of seven-star hotels and admiring their picturesque views, dining in Michelin-starred restaurants sometimes alone and sometimes with other notable personalities in the business space. He created good content and his audience lived for it, Ewa being one of his avid followers. That day, in April of 2020, he'd posted a story of himself sitting alone in a gondola in Venice at dawn, captioning it *#Serenity*. Ewa had commented *I could do with a little bit of that now*. He often ignored messages and comments from people he didn't know, but something made him not only click on her message, but her profile page as well. The first picture he'd seen was one of her in a twirl in some kind of garden, her floaty, rainbow-patterned skirt at one with the vibrant colours of the surrounding flowers. Her face was not in focus, but something about the carefree way her hands were held up fascinated him. The next picture was a close-up shot of her face as she looked back at the camera, her eyes wide and questioning, her lips parted as if in mid-sentence. Staring at that picture, he'd been captivated by her large eyes, eyes that drew him in the longer he looked. By the time he saw the third picture, one of her on a yacht, in a skimpy bikini that showcased her slender body with its pert breasts and narrow hips, and not the voluptuous, almost cartoonish, often surgically enhanced bodies that had become the norm on social media, he found himself intrigued by her. So, he'd replied her message. *Maybe next time I'm going, you can come ;-)*.

And the rest was history.

At thirty-four, he was ready for marriage, and after meeting her in person a little over a week later, he'd decided she was perfect for him. Thankfully, it was a reciprocated feeling and they fell in love, with him proposing about a year later.

But in the last few months, apart from getting increasingly rankled by her frivolity and financial irresponsibility, he has started desiring something much deeper than a superficial kind of love.

"Seriously, babe," he says, pulling her closer. "You look more beautiful without all this. Have you forgotten how I couldn't take my eyes off you the first time I visited you at your parents' house in Osogbo?"

Flashbacks of their first Christmas together flood his head, when he paid her a surprise visit at her parents' home in South Western Nigeria. He smiles at the memory of her opening the door, wearing nothing but a t-shirt and shorts, her hair in knotless braids wrapped in a loose bun on top of her head. That was the day he knew he was in love with her, the day he knew he would marry her.

"Let's get married there," he says, his face brightening at the idea.

"Where?"

"Osogbo!" he expounds, grinning. "It would be much more convenient for your parents, your dad especially." Her father has been confined to a wheelchair since a stroke in 2017. "And the view from their backyard is absolutely amazing." With their compound sloping into a neighbour's extensive cassava plantation, the lush rows of green plants from the farm combined with the distant view of Ado Hill make for a breathtaking view. "We could have a more intimate ceremony there, away from all the Lagos stress and *wahala*."

THE MARRIAGE CLASS

Ewa blinks once, and then twice, in complete disbelief over what she has just heard. Get married in Osogbo? How? And their wedding being less than four months away isn't the only reason the mere suggestion has left her flabbergasted. Getting married there is completely out of the question.

"It might cost a bit more to transport our vendors there, but it can be done. Thankfully, Logan Hall has a full refund policy if we cancel before ninety days," he continues, his excitement building.

Her lips part as she watches him talk, realizing he isn't joking.

"Babe, you're serious?" she laughs. "You, Sanya Wellington, want to get married in Osogbo? Hashtag #CheersToTheWellingtons happening in Osogbo?" She shakes her head and pulls out of his embrace. "You better go back to sleep, as I can see you're still dreaming."

He watches her walk to the bed, and his frown deepens. "Why does getting married in your hometown amuse you?"

"You think your friends are going to go all the way to Osogbo? Your high-profile business buddies, you think they'll come?"

"Our close friends and family will, and that's what really matters."

"*Abeg, abeg*, Sanya," she waves a dismissive hand as she reaches for her phone. "Do you think I spent eighteen thousand dollars on an Oscar de la Renta gown, and over a million naira on a Matopeda reception gown, for 'close friends and family'? And the crystal chandeliers Ndidi is flying in just for the day? All that to entertain awon *alapata elede* and *agbe*? Don't be ridiculous."

He stands there, staggered to hear her dresses combined have cost well over ten-million-naira. He watches her for several minutes as she scrolls through her phone, the annoying feathered lashes fluttering with every blink, and he feels the most estranged from her he ever has.

"What is more important to you, Ewa?" he finally asks. "Making an impression and showing off to the whole world, or celebrating our love?"

"Says the man who takes pictures in first class, for the 'gram,'" she scoffs, not even looking up at him. "Don't be a hypocrite, Sanya. You want an Internet-breaking wedding just as much as I do."

A year, maybe even a few months, before, that might have been the case. But now, these things no longer matter. And he realizes the problem isn't where they will, or will not, have the wedding.

But that these things still matter to her.

4. THE COUGAR

Roles & Responsibilities

Kris & Bola

Kris stands before the wall-mounted mirror in her hallway and gives herself a once-over, pleased with the fit of the terracotta orange bodycon dress, hoisting up her breasts with her hands even though the full globes of flesh need no further uplift. Eyeing the tattoo of her name that runs across her collarbone, she tilts her head, wondering if displaying it for their church appointment will be appropriate. Deciding covering it will be better, she pulls up her sleeves from where they rest below her shoulders, bringing them up to its slopes. The tattoo isn't fully covered, but it isn't shouting *hello* to onlookers either. The honk of a horn reminds her she should be out of the door, and, smacking together her scarlet red lips, she flicks off the light switch, walks out the door, turns the key in the lock three times, and, smiling, heads to the Toyota Camry purring in her driveway.

"Hi, handsome," she says, winking at Bola, who is at the wheel.

He reaches over and she leans into him, their lips fusing in a lock that is every bit as heated, every bit as passionate, as the first time they kissed. "Hello, gorgeous," he says, when they pull apart.

She smiles and looks at her watch. "Class four, huh? Let's go do this thing."

"The issue of roles and responsibilities in any kind of relationship, not just a marriage, is a very fluid and relative one," Ifeyinwa says, her loud voice carrying through the class. "In marriage, it is often a conflict between what society expects," she lifts one hand, "and what the couple wants," she raises her other hand, to reflect the dichotomy.

Her eyes sweep the class and they land on the man engaged to the older woman. "Kris, what do you believe a man's role in a marriage should be?"

"*I'm* Kris," his partner says, leaning forward with a flat palm on her chest. "He's Bola."

THE MARRIAGE CLASS

I look at her, her lips vibrant in red and her tight dress hugging a body that is in better shape than mine, and I can understand why she would be attractive to a younger man. Heck, she would be attractive to a man of any age.

"Even their names are confused about who will wear the pants!" comes a stage whisper from the back of the class, followed by loud chuckling.

I turn around and see the guy with the afro, Boma I think is his name, laughing along with the guy with the thick Igbo accent, and I feel like giving them two backhand slaps, one for each of them.

"Don't be fooled by his quiet demeanor," Kris says, her lips upturned in a coy smile. "Bola definitely 'wears the pants' in our relationship."

I grimace. Was that really necessary? My eyes drift to Bola's face, and if his clenched jaw is anything to go by, I'm not the only one who thinks his babe would have been better off ignoring the hecklers at the back.

But who am I to question them?

Thirty minutes later, as the class takes a short break, as Raymond chats in a group with some of the guys, I reach for my phone, clicking on the LinkedIn app for the umpteenth time, eager to see which of our mutual acquaintances have commented on Lucas's job announcement post. I read his new title yet again, examine every nuance and detail of his profile picture yet again, read the congratulatory messages yet again. And I decide to add one of my own - a congratulatory message. I might as well, I guess.

Nice one on the new job. Congratulations.

Hitting the *send* button, I bite my nails, staring at my message as it joins the over one hundred comments on the post.

Roles and responsibilities. It's amazing how roles can evolve in relationships. How someone can go from being a boyfriend…to a fiancé…to an ex.

The vibration of my phone makes me start, and my eyes widen when I see a notification that Lucas has sent me a private message.

Thanks for the good wishes, babe. How are you?

Shaken, I toss my phone into my bag, looking around to be sure nobody is close enough to have read the message.

Or read anything from my face, either.

Kris & Bola

"Some of the guys in that class are so uncouth," Kris remarks, as their car connects with the Third Mainland Bridge from Herbert Macaulay Way. "And it's the older ones who should know better, too."

THE MARRIAGE CLASS

Bola purses his lips, determined not to get into an argument about it. "Next time, ignore them."

She shrugs and smiles as DJ Tunez's *Pami* starts to play from the radio. "I love this song."

Kris nods and rolls her shoulders in sync with the music and Bola can't help the smile that forms on his face as he steals a glance at her. Her natural hair is in twists that frame her face, and in the glow of the streetlights, she looks ethereal.

"Have you put your house up for sale yet?" he asks.

The smile on her face vanishes and the rolling of her shoulders ceases. It is a reaction he expected, but it is a conversation that must be had...now that they still have time.

"Why do you keep insisting on this?" she asks, her voice clipped. "How do you expect me to commute all the way from Ajah to my gallery every day?"

"Ikoyi is just about an hour away," Bola answers, stealing another glance at her. "It's not that far, babe."

"An hour away in dreamland or where?" Kris retorts. "When was the last time it took you an hour to get to town?" She exhales and places her hand on his arm. "Honey, my place is bigger, more central, and, most importantly, not rented. Why can't you just move in with me? It will make life so much easier for us both."

He snaps his head in her direction. "How can you even ask that? You want me to move in with you and solidify this toy boy impression people have of me? You want to fan the flames of gossip? You heard those guys laughing in class, didn't you?"

"You knew it would be like this, Bola," she answers through clenched teeth, taking her hand off his arm and pulling back. "You knew what you were getting into before asking me to marry you. I didn't ask for any of this. You're the one who insisted we could make it work."

He turns to look at her and their eyes hold; hers in defiance and his…in distress.

From the moment he saw her that first time, at an art exhibition in June of 2021, he'd lost his head and heart to her. A friend of his had invited him for the much talked about exhibition of an upcoming artist who liked to express their non-binary identification through art. Bola had been looking at the portrait of a cross between an androgynous female and a femme man, half of its body chiseled and ripped, with a hand cupping a large breast, and the other side, an effeminate albeit bearded face, framed by long, flowing hair, the other hand cupping a large pair of male genitalia.

"That's also my favourite one. Very intriguing," a silky voice had come from behind him, confident yet gentle, giving him the feeling of his ear being massaged with a soothing, yet arousing, balm.

THE MARRIAGE CLASS

Turning in the direction of the voice, the response he wanted to give about how he found the painting more disturbing than intriguing, evaporated from his lips as he beheld the woman standing there. In a free form, floor-length, chiffon dress in bright red, black, and white *adire* print, *kente* patterned wooden bangles stacked wrist to elbow on both hands, her hair in bantu knots, twin diamond piercings above each nostril, a half-hoop through her septum, and wide eyes lined a vibrant green, she took his breath away.

"That good?" she'd laughed, a sound that crinkled her eyes. "You like it that much, it's left you speechless?"

"No, ma'am," he'd answered, recovering his composure. "I like *you* that much."

Cheesy though it was, it had gotten her attention, and she'd agreed to his request to take her out for drinks after the exhibition. As they chatted and laughed over several glasses of Old Fashioned and Whisky Sour, they discovered a shared love of art, what with her being a curator and him, a sculptor. He'd shown her pictures of his work and she'd scribbled on a piece of paper phone numbers of galleries looking to showcase bronze casted sculptures.

But as the night progressed, it was clear that art wasn't on the forefront of either of their minds. From the way their eyes held, to the lingering touch of her hand on his as she listened to him talk, to the brush of his cheek on hers when he leaned in to speak when the music got louder, there was a definite crackle – actually, more like a blast - of electricity between them.

"I live not too far from here," she'd said, a pointed look in her eyes as he paid for their drinks.

She had noticed him when he walked into the gallery, and nothing about his closely cropped hair, simple blue button-down shirt, dark blue jeans, and black trainers had given him away as an artist. But the more he spoke, she found herself seduced not just by the depth of his knowledge about, and love for, art, but the richness of his voice, smooth and sensual like auditory caramel. And she was in no hurry to say goodnight.

Holding her eyes, he understood the invitation for what it was, and accepted it without a second thought, driving her the few streets that separated the bar from her house on Raymond Njoku Street. Even though he'd suspected she was a little older, more because of the people she named as her contemporaries than anything, walking into the exquisitely furnished detached house she called hers, confirmed this suspicion. But as she pulled him into her arms, none of that even mattered. All he wanted to do was lose himself in the passion that was now fever pitch high with the kind of intensity that would have made it impossible to stop.

Except he didn't even want to stop.

As they kissed, as he stripped her of her clothes, as she did the same for him, as their bodies fused in a oneness that felt innate, he knew it was special. He knew it was no one-off.

For her, even though the sex was amazing, even though his touch ignited every nerve and sensory ending in her body like none ever had, she hadn't thought more of it than a casual hook-up, of which she'd had quite a few. After a nine-year relationship ended abruptly the year she turned thirty-four, and after spending more than a few years chasing several mirages, trying to force things that weren't, at thirty-nine, she'd accepted that marriage probably wouldn't be in the offing for her. It had been liberating to emancipate herself from the chokehold that was her desperation to settle down, and, instead, release herself to enjoy life. And so she had fallen in love with herself, thrown herself into the art world that was her passion, and now, at age forty-four, she had learned how to be the one thing she'd never given herself liberty to in the past; selfishly happy.

But when one night with Bola led to several others, one evening to several months, his earnestness, sincerity, and unabashed love for her wore down her defenses. Despite how hard she tried to keep her heart safe in its cage, he had somehow been able to find the key.

But now, sitting with him in the car, she starts to wish she'd been more careful with that key.

"When we got engaged, I told you, Bola," she says, returning her eyes to the Lagos skyline stretched before them as the car races down the bridge. "I told you society isn't ready for a love like ours and that there will always be talk. If it isn't talk about you living with me, or even me living with you, it'll be about whether or not I can give you kids, or how long you'll stick around before deciding I'm too old for you anyway."

"Kris..."

"I don't think you have the kind of thick skin you need to be with an older woman," she cuts in, turning to look at him.

As their eyes hold, the weight of her statement, the reminder that their marriage might be just as bad in reality as it is on paper, sits heavy between them.

"Are you okay in there?"

At the sound of Raymond's voice, I look up from where I sit on the toilet. Since getting to his apartment a little under an hour ago, I have been here - in the toilet - the whole time.

"I'm fine," I shout back. "I'll soon be out."

Satisfied I have allayed his fears about what is keeping me here so long, I smile as my fingers dance across my phone's keypad, replying another message from Lucas. All through class and even the ride back to Raymond's place, I could hardly focus, my mind on my phone, which kept chiming with incoming messages. Once in the flat, I'd made a dash to the toilet and grinned when I saw twelve - a whole *twelve* - messages from Lucas, messages with questions about how I am, how I have been in the three years since our breakup, questions about everything from my family members, to work…to Raymond.

For real? You got engaged to that guy? I didn't know you liked nerds, is his last message.

He's not a nerd. He's a lovely guy, I reply, my smile broadening.

Lovely guy? Are you describing your fiancé or your teacher? I hope he knows how lucky he is to have an amazing woman like you. Something I wish I knew then.

I sigh and press the phone to my chest, lightheaded after reading what I have so desperately wanted to hear since our acrimonious breakup.

Roles and responsibilities. How quickly these can change! How quickly an ex can become…a lover?

5. BEAUTY AND THE BEAST

Intimacy

Chioma & A.K.

Chioma wipes off her lipstick with a wet wipe and reaches for a dark brown liner, running the pencil around the border of lips again, emphasizing the Cupid's bow the way the YouTube tutorial showed. Reapplying the bright red lipstick, she frowns at her reflection in the mirror, the severe brown and red mishmash making her look like an extra from a 1980's Herbert Ogunde movie, hers nothing like the perfect red lips sported by the woman in their marriage class she'd wanted to copy. Rather than achieve Kris's striking and sensual look, all she has ended up with are clown-like lips that look even larger than they already are.

"Sweetness, are you ready? We'll be late."

She sighs upon hearing A.K.'s voice. So much for wanting to look more attractive than she typically does…knowing using the word *attractive* is being generous.

"I'll be right out," she calls out, wiping off the red lipstick for the fifth time that evening, adding to the dull hue of red that has formed in the space between her lower lip and her chin. She grabs another wet wipe to attack the area, rubbing vigorously but only succeeding in peeling open a recently healed blackhead. Glaring at the now bleeding spot, she throws the wipe into the wastebasket by her foot, the blackhead healed no more. Sighing again, she takes out from her makeup bag the pale pink lipstick she has used for years and which, with the right amount of liner, makes her lips look smaller, more passable.

Except she was hoping for more than passable today, something that would attract less curious and bemused stares from the people in their marriage class. Heck, from anyone that sees her and A.K. together. She applies her long-trusted lipstick, slicks on the usual layer of gloss, and, staring at her reflection in the mirror, squints to make her large eyes lose some of their bulk, and purses her lips to make them lose some of their volume. But her overlapping teeth give her mouth the appearance of a bird's beak, and her eyes look like she is missing some very strongly recommended medicated glasses.

ADESUWA O'MAN NWOKEDI

What is A.K. doing with a girl like her?

It's a question she has asked herself since their relationship crossed the line over a year ago, when she went from being just his travel agent…to his lover. Even before meeting him, every time he'd called to book a ticket, she got butterflies in her stomach hearing his voice. A notorious playboy, even though most of his travel was for business, a good many of these trips were holidays with whomever was his romantic interest at the time, and Chioma had been on hand to book those flights. She didn't meet him in person for the first eighteen months of working at the agency, but, even though she had an idea what he looked like from the picture on his passport's data page, when he'd walked into their agency himself, to resolve a problem with a multi-destination booking, she'd melted. As he'd chatted and joked with everyone in the room, she saw that even his good looks were no match for his charm.

"Ah, Chioma the magician!" he had exclaimed, shaking her hand, his grin revealing a deep cleft in his chin. "The woman with the magic wand, able to get me any seat I want at any time. It's great to finally meet you."

She'd barely been able to manage a coherent response, stuttering and unable to hold eye contact. He hadn't noticed her discomfort and soon moved on to greet her other colleagues.

They didn't see each other for another year. In April 2021, while at a beach resort on the outskirts of town, celebrating a friend's husband's fortieth birthday, A.K. walked into the elevator she was riding down to the lobby to meet her group.

"Chioma, the magician!" he exclaimed. "What are you doing here?"

She flushed, equal parts self-aware of the tight t-shirt she wore - monogrammed for the celebrant and a size too small – over short shorts that exposed her thick thighs, and flattered that he even recognized her. "I'm here for a birthday party." Feeling uncharacteristically brazen, she smiled at him. "You?"

"Well, also here for a birthday, except it's mine," he chuckled. "Only difference being that I'm here alone. It's a ritual I have, an annual solo retreat before every birthday to meditate."

"Oh, interesting."

He laughed, a sound that uncaged a profusion of butterflies in her stomach. "I know that look. Many people don't understand why I come all this way every year." He shrugged. "But this one in particular is especially important. It's the last year of my thirties and I desperately need to take stock of my life." The lift doors opened and he smiled at her. "Anyway, enjoy your party."

Disappointed their brief conversation was over, but grateful nonetheless it had happened, she raised her hand in a wave. "Happy meditating. And happy birthday in advance."

She'd walked only a few paces when he called her name.

"If your party is over early, maybe we could have a drink or something?" he asked. "After two nights alone, I guess I'm craving some company."

She was nodding even before he finished talking. "Sure. I'd like that. Let me give you my number."

"I already have it," he answered, his smile disarming her. "You've forgotten how I blew up your lines - yours and Bukola's - that time my connecting flight out of Sao Paulo was cancelled and I needed to be on another one to make my meeting in Miami the next day?"

"I remember," she chuckled.

"I promise I won't talk about anything concerning tickets, flights, miles, or luggage allowance," he said, raising a hand as if taking an oath.

She laughed again, feeling more and more at ease. Even if he did, she wouldn't mind at all. "I have your number as well, so I'll call you."

And call him she did. As soon as her friend's husband cut his cake, Chioma made an excuse to leave and was dialing A.K.'s number even before she left the group, joining him at the bar where he was nursing a cocktail. Sitting with him, what started as small talk about banal things like how crunchy the served peanuts were, to the crippling traffic leading to the resort as a result of road works, soon led to them talking about their lives, families, careers, hopes, and dreams. He told her about feeling disenchanted with the life he lived and desperately wanting to give back to society, and she told him about growing up an orphan and having to fend for her siblings from the early age of seventeen. They talked through the night, changing location from the bar when it closed at 3am, to sit on the beach under the moonlight, talking until sunrise.

Mindful of her group's 8am departure time, they had to cut their conversation short, and he walked her to the door of room.

"I had a wonderful time, Chioma," he said.

"Me too," she answered, regretful their magical time had come to an end, but under no illusion it would continue when they left the resort and returned to the real world. "Happy birthday in adv…"

His lips on hers silenced her, and she melted in his arms like ice cream on a hot waffle, yielding as his mouth explored hers, soft and tender, but yet probing.

It took all his willpower to pull away from her, and he stared at her just as surprised by the kiss as she was. After briefly contemplating an apology, he decided against it. Because, though unplanned, he felt no penitence at all. "Bye, Chioma."

"Bye," she said, lowering her eyes as she swiped her card key, opened the door, and disappeared into the room.

Walking in the direction of the elevator, A.K. was unable to wipe off the smile that had formed on his face, unable to remember the last time a conversation with any woman had left him feeling the way he was - unburdened, energized, excited. And for the rest of the day, resonating in his head were images of her listening intently as he spoke, and laughing as they bantered. The feel of her hand on his in silent support as he bared his soul, lingered, and the floral scent of her natural hair as he held her as she cried while telling him about her late parents, still pervaded his senses.

He was captivated by her.

Back at work the next day, Chioma was surprised to receive a large bouquet of red roses from him.

Let's do it again. Dinner tonight? A.K.

She laughed at the straight-to-the-point message, calling him even before the delivery man left her office. "How can we have dinner when you're still at Epe? Your birthday is tomorrow, isn't it?"

"I decided to leave early. I'd rather spend my birthday with you."

And with those words, he won her heart.

Dinner that night led to breakfast the following morning, and even though, given his reputation, she knew she was taking a gamble, she fell head over heels in love with him, his reciprocity of her feelings making it so much sweeter and almost making up for the strange looks they got anytime they were out together.

Almost.

She tried not to notice all the attention A.K. got from men and women alike, and the raised brows, parted mouths, and heads cocked to the side as, she was certain, they tried to figure out what she was to him. Because a man like him most surely could not have her as a girlfriend.

"Chioma, we'll be late!" A.K.'s voice brings her back to reality.

"I'll be right out," she shouts, gathering her makeup, new and old, into the vanity case she brought along.

Red lipstick or no, people in their class will just have to accept her the way she is.

"Today's topic is intimacy," Maxwell begins the class, saying. "And its importance in this journey you are all about to take; the journey called marriage." His eyes scan the class. "And intimacy isn't only physical. It's not just about sex. It's also emotional, intellectual, and even spiritual."

The class is pin drop silent, everyone is listening with rapt attention.

"I'm throwing this question to the men," Maxwell continues. "How did you know your fiancée was *the one*?"

A.K.'s hand shoots up and, like I am every week, I am fascinated by how proud this handsome specimen of a man is of his love for a woman many men wouldn't even look at once, let alone twice. It's amazing, really.

"Yes, A.K." Maxwell nods in his direction.

A.K. rises to his feet. "I went most of my life thinking I'd never want to lay roots and settle down with anyone." He turns to his fiancée and smiles. "Even before I met Chioma face to face, I was enthralled by her laughter, captivated by the sound of her voice. When I met her in person, I fell in love with her smile, her dancing eyes, her sense of humour." He winks at her. "Her insane body." His smile wanes but his eyes remain on her. "And the fact that I can talk to her for hours, that I can share with her everything, without shame or reproach. She is home for me, and when I realized that, I knew she was the one."

I cross my arms and watch them with a gaping jaw, still unable to wrap my mind around this odd and unlikely couple. And I can't help but wonder if there is a *beauty and the beast* element with every couple.

My phone vibrates and I see it is a message from Lucas. Flashing Raymond a quick glance to be certain he hasn't seen it, I turn my phone face down.

Maybe *I'm* the beast in this relationship.

THE MARRIAGE CLASS

Chioma & A.K.

Chioma shifts from one foot to the other as A.K. chats with Ewa, answering questions she has about a campaign she is hoping to run for Moët & Chandon, having discovered A.K.'s close relationship with its Country Manager. As Ewa laughs over something he has said, Chioma's chest tightens, intimidated. In a belted shirt dress, a shiny bone straight wig, and flawlessly applied makeup complete with glossy lips in the same shade of red Chioma earlier struggled with, Ewa looks effortlessly glamorous.

And the inadequacy Chioma feels chokes her.

"That Ewa sure had a lot to say," she says later that evening, as they walk into A.K.'s Victoria Island apartment.

"All these influencers and their hang ups," he chuckles in response, walking into the kitchen, opening the fridge and bringing out a can of soda. "But you can't blame her for being desperate to win back Moët's account. I hear they pay them very well."

"She's very beautiful," Chioma says, keen eyes on him. "You two looked very good together."

He pops open the drink and takes a long sip, before he turns to her. "Let's not do this again, sweetness. I thought we agreed last time would be the last time."

A few weeks before, convinced she was the subject of discussion amongst his aunties at his cousin's wedding, she had broken down on their way home, and it had taken him days to convince her that not only was it unlikely his aunties had been talking about her, but that, even if they had, he had made it clear to his family that he had chosen *her*, and that was the most important thing. Appeased, she'd promised never to bring it up in discussion ever again.

A promise she has now broken after less than a month.

"A.K., let's stop lying to ourselves," she says, shaking her head. "That's the kind of woman people expect you to be with."

"Didn't you hear a word I said in class?" he asks, setting down the soda can. "What kind of foolish talk is this, Chioma?"

"Every single person we have ever come across wonders what you see in me."

"Why the fuck should I be bothered what people *wonder* I see in you when I *know* what I do?"

A lump rises in her throat and she pinches her forehead to keep from crying. "It's getting too much for me, A.K. It's getting too much. I'm tired of constantly trying to do everything to look and sound a certain way when we're together. Trying - to no avail I might add - to make the staring from strangers stop. And I'm tired. I'm tired, A.K."

"So, what are you saying, Chioma?" he asks, after they have stood in silence for a full minute. "What exactly are you saying?"

She looks up at him, and is unable to speak the words her inner saboteur is screaming loudly in her ear.

6. INTERNATIONAL BOO

Communication

My doorbell rings as I am slipping on a pair of three-inch pumps, in my preparation for this evening's class. I was able to leave work early enough today, easier with it being a Friday.

Looking through the peephole, I am surprised to see Raymond standing outside, especially as we didn't make any plans to ride to Yaba together. Especially as we haven't made any plans since the last time I was with him on Monday.

"Was it the fish?" he'd asked, when I finally emerged from the toilet that night.

THE MARRIAGE CLASS

"The fish?"

"The fish from lunch this afternoon. I remember thinking it didn't taste that fresh. Is that what upset your stomach?" he'd asked again. "You were in there a while."

"Yeah, yeah, the fish," I'd answered, nodding emphatically. "It really did a number on me."

"My poor baby," he'd said, pulling me closer. "What can I do to make it better? I could brew you a cup of ginger tea?"

I'd looked up at him and a lump formed in my throat, because of the gratitude I felt for the love of this beautiful and kind man…and the guilt I was awash with for wishing it was another man holding me.

"Ginger tea sounds good," was what I managed to answer, dropping my eyes, unable to sustain eye contact lest he saw in them everything I'd texted Lucas in the past hour.

The ginger tea was just as good as promised. Rich and soothing, it was healing to both my bogus unsettled stomach and the ache in my conflicted heart, conflicted even more as we kissed, as his lips teased mine, light and gentle in the beginning, and dark and deep as his body demanded more of mine, and mine, more of his. But as his sensual kisses trailed my body, as our bodies moved in rhythmic unison, unlike every other time when I was unable to think of anything else, I couldn't keep my eyes from drifting to my bag, the intermittent flashes of light the indicator that Lucas was sending more messages. Later that night, as he held me in a tight cuddle, I was not lulled to sleep by the usual afterglow endorphins or calmed by the smell that was the combination of his perfume and masculine aroma. Instead, all night, I found myself longing…yearning…to read what else Lucas had written me.

Which was why, when Raymond suggested lunch the following day, I declined. I did the same when he asked me to come over to his place the next day, having a bag full of excuses every day - cramps on Tuesday, an extended team meeting on Wednesday, drinks with a random girlfriend on Thursday - not wanting to be anywhere I would be unable to continue the flirtatious text exchange with my ex-fiancé. I thought I'd been convincing, but now, if the look on Raymond's face is anything to go by, I guess not quite convincing enough.

"Hey," I say to him, when I open the door, smiling.

He doesn't return my smile. "Abi, we need to talk."

The smile on my face freezes when I hear those dreaded words *we need to talk*.

Communication.

It is the easiest, and also the hardest, thing any couple has to do.

THE MARRIAGE CLASS

Bianca & Prince

"Babes, I can't hear you," Bianca calls out, switching the phone from one ear to the other, in between glancing at the screen to check the connectivity status of the call. When she sees the *reconnecting* sign, she sighs and leans back in the seat of the taxi ferrying her from Lagos Island, where she went to deliver supplies to a new signee of her parents, to Yaba for marriage class.

Surely, it shouldn't be this hard to have a simple conversation.

"Can you hear me now?" Prince's voice cuts in. "I thought you said switching from video to voice would improve the quality of the call."

Well, clearly, it didn't. Do I look like MTN? she is tempted to retort, but she purses her lips instead.

"Are you almost at the church?" he asks. "My classes here are going very well, have I told you? The Priest has been so insightful. He's been counseling couples for almost forty years, so you can imagine how much he…"

"We need to fix a date, Prince," Bianca cuts in, her frustration more from the open-endedness of their engagement than the poor network. "When are you coming back? How can I be attending marriage class when I don't even..."

The *reconnecting* beep sounds again and she growls as she throws the phone in her handbag, ignoring the curious look from the Uber driver, feeling so frustrated she wants to fling her handbag out the window, over the bridge and into the lagoon - the bag and the wretched, cheerless phone it contains.

"Communication in any relationship is very important, no matter the kind of relationship it is," Maxwell says, weaving his way through the class. "It is essential, critical even, to share everything with your partner; the good, the bad and the ugly."

During a break, Raymond turns to me. "Can we talk now?"

Before leaving my house, I managed to convince him that talking would make us late for class, and got him to agree to not only postpone this discussion, but for us to ride separately to class. Even though I would have loved any opportunity not to drive myself to the mainland, riding with him was out of the question, considering I'd committed myself to other plans for later...

THE MARRIAGE CLASS

"Raymond, how can we talk here in class?" I ask, my eyes darting around. "Besides, you know this break is only for ten minutes."

"It won't take long."

"Let's talk after class," I say, covering his hand with mine. "I'll come to your place later."

"Why don't I just drive behind you straight to yours?"

"I have an errand to run." It's a lie. "For my mother." It's another lie. But I can only afford to tell him lies.

Because I simply cannot tell him the truth.

Bianca & Prince

Bianca blows her cheeks in her frustration as the call rings out yet again. She glances at the clock on the wall and, at 11pm, 6pm in Toronto, Prince should be on his commute from work to the home where he tutors. Surely, he should be able to answer her call, at least.

I've been trying to reach you, she types, mouthing the words as her fingers tap on the keys of her phone. *Call me back. It's urgent.*

She sits, one eye on the clock and the other on her phone, willing the latter to ring before it is midnight on the former, because at 7pm Toronto time, Prince will be unavailable for another two hours.

"Are you sure this guy doesn't have a wife and kids in that Canada?" Toyosi, her childhood friend, had asked earlier that day, when Bianca was unable to give her a firm date for the wedding. "First, he disappointed you last Christmas after promising he would come. Then he couldn't even be bothered to come for your introduction. *Na picture im people bring come your house!*"

"He hasn't been able to get his P.R., I already told you."

"All this while?" Toyosi exclaimed. "In two years? Not even now that you have actually started attending marriage class? *Abi* is it a picture you'll exchange vows with at the altar? Bianca, you have never set your eyes on this man for a single day. This doesn't sound right one bit."

Looking at the clock as it its long hand meets its short one at the numeral twelve, it doesn't sound right to Bianca either. And she starts to wonder why she ever thought it was a good idea.

She'd been in her final year of university when a lady approached her in church. A beautiful and elegantly dressed woman she had admired from afar for several Sundays, Bianca was flattered by the woman's interest.

"I've been watching you for a while," the lady, Doris as she introduced herself, said as they sat alone on a pew at the end of Mass. "It's very rare to see a young, beautiful girl like you so devout. There hasn't been a single Sunday that I haven't seen you here. I have asked after you from several people, and not one person has had a bad word to say about you. From the church wardens to members of Block Rosary, everyone has praised you for being courteous, friendly, well-behaved, and, very importantly, patient with the kids in the crusade."

Bianca smiled, humbled by the praise, but also confused why the woman would feel the need to tell her all that.

"I told my sisters about you. I even sent them your picture," Doris smiled, raising her phone and showing Bianca a picture taken from the previous year's harvest and bazaar program. "And we all agree that you'll be perfect for our brother."

The frown on Bianca's face was involuntary. Perfect for whom?

Doris must have picked up on her hesitancy as she smiled, covering her hand with hers. "I know it might not be something that will interest a young girl like you. Just talk to him. Allow me give him your number so you two can talk. That's all I'm asking."

Deciding there was no harm in that, Bianca punched her number into the woman's phone, and, that very evening, she'd gotten the call. Making up her mind to indulge the man in one conversation and one conversation only, she hadn't been prepared for the deep, almost hypnotic voice that came through when she answered her phone.

"Hello. Is this Bianca? My name is Prince."

The way he pronounced her name was almost lyrical, dragging the last syllable of her name in an endless *aaah*.

"Hi, Prince. Yes, this is Bianca," she answered, unable to stop the accompanying giggle.

"Biancaaah," he said, a smile in his voice. "The name of the first woman I ever had a crush on; Bianca Onoh, or rather, Bianca Ojukwu." He laughed, a throaty sound that prompted more laughter from her, even though she had no idea what the heck they were laughing about. "I guess I just gave my age away calling her by her maiden name."

She leaned into her pillow, the smile on her face broadening. "Not exactly."

"Biancas are always very beautiful."

"Ah, but there are levels oh," she chuckled. "Ambassador Bianca Ojukwu and I are not on the same level at all!"

"No, you're way more beautiful."

Even though she knew it was the highest possible extent of flattery, she'd covered her mouth to contain the bubble of giggles erupting from her stomach. Like Renée Zellweger's character in the movie *Jerry Maguire* had said to Tom Cruise's, Prince had her at *hello*.

They spoke for two hours that day, with him telling her how he had quit his job with an engineering company in Lagos three years before, to relocate to Canada, and her telling him about growing up the first of six children and juggling school with working with her parents in their network marketing business with a global supplements brand. After the call, she'd lain in bed with a dreamy smile on her face, his alluring baritone voice resonating in her head, unable to wait for the next time he would call again.

He didn't call for another two weeks.

As the days went by without her phone lighting up with a call from him, she ran herself crazy, analyzing everything she had said during that first conversation, wondering what she had done to put him off, worried he had decided she wasn't worth wasting his time on. She had been close to caving and calling Doris to ask if her brother had told her anything, when his call came early on a Sunday morning. Bianca's heart had almost exploded from sheer joy when she'd seen his name on her screen, having already saved his number as *My Prince*.

"It's 2am here, and I was going to call you later in the day," had been his opener, "but I couldn't wait to hear your voice again."

"Well, you waited two weeks." It was out of her mouth before she could stop it, realizing in hindsight just how eager it made her sound.

"I was scared I came on too strong last time, so I wanted to give you some space," he answered. "But you have been my sleeping and waking thought, Bianca. I have looked at the picture on your DP so many times, I can draw it from memory."

The blouse she was ironing for church forgotten, she sat on her bed, her cheeks aching from smiling, but restraining herself from letting him know it had been the same for her.

"I like you, Bianca. When my sisters told me they had someone for me, I didn't believe them. But after speaking with you…" His voice trailed off for a few seconds. "This is serious for me, Bianca. I want to pursue something serious with you."

And it was music to her ears.

The more they talked, the more they ticked each other's boxes, and by the end of their first month of active discussions, talking to him every day had become an integral, non-negotiable part of her life.

Even though she'd been disappointed not knowing how soon she would see him face to face, he'd made up for it by spoiling her with gifts sent through his sisters and anyone he found coming to Lagos, and sending her money before she even asked. She wanted for nothing and soon no longer worried about how long their relationship was stretching without any physical contact, not even a first one. She was satisfied with their daily video calls, the surprise gifts, the bank alerts that came at the right time, and didn't feel any need to pressure him about the continued postponements of his trip to Nigeria. Not even when he formally proposed, not even when he sent her a website link to pick her engagement ring, not even when his sisters, aged father, and relatives had come for the perfunctory introduction ceremony with only a picture to represent him.

THE MARRIAGE CLASS

But now, with no end in sight to their unconventional arrangement, she is no longer satisfied. As a matter of fact, she is far from it. And it is why she stays up until he gets off work at 2am Nigeria time to call him again, directly via her mobile network this time, and not the Internet calls that are their norm.

"Sweetness, what are you still doing awake" he asks, his voice raised in his surprise. "I saw your message but it was too late to call…"

"What exactly is keeping you in Canada, Prince?" she cuts in. "People who started working on their P.R. long before you have since gotten theirs. You proposed to me months ago and haven't even as much as given my parents a date to start planning towards? Or is your plan to detain me with this ring? To tie me down for years? I'm not *Lord of the Rings* oh!"

"Detain you? Bianca, you know the issues I'm having with my P.R."

"How am I sure you don't have a wife over there in Canada? Maybe even kids. How am I sure your sisters didn't catch me for you as your home based wife, while you live happily with your real family in Toronto?"

Silence stretches and she has to look at her phone to be sure the line hasn't disconnected, regretting not having called via WhatsApp video, wishing she can see the reaction on his face, a reaction she is certain is guilt.

"My real family in Toronto," he finally mutters, repeating the last part of her diatribe. "I didn't know you think so little of me, Bianca."

"Then prove me wrong!" she yells, not caring if she rouses her sleeping household. "Come here, so I can see the man I have committed to marry. Let me touch your skin. Let me smell your body odour. Let us fight about who sleeps on what side of the bed. Prove me wrong by giving me a definite date, Prince!"

"If you are so wary, call it off," he says, his voice flat. "If you think I'm deceiving you, that I'm taking you for a ride, call this engagement off!"

Her shoulders sag and her mouth parts, his response not one she expected. Still holding the phone, she catches her reflection in the mirror, the diamond ring on her finger glinting in the darkness of the room, and her stomach sinks as she watches her dream implode before her eyes.

My eyes dart around the pub I haven't set foot in in over three years, empty except for four people seated; three of them a group of friends on the same table, and the fourth, alone nursing his drink.

The fourth being Lucas.

He spots me and raises his hand in a wave, standing at the same time. My heart thumps hard in my chest when I see

THE MARRIAGE CLASS

him, tall and beautiful with his work shirt rolled at the sleeves, showing of his hairy forearms. I return his wave and make my way where he is, in the same corner booth that was once our spot, the spot where we would sit, drinking beer and watching football as we waited for traffic headed to the mainland to abate, so he could take me home. Apart from no longer needing to wait anywhere for rush hour traffic to abate since I now live on the island, there is that pertinent detail that we are no longer a couple. He is married to someone else…and I'm engaged to Raymond.

Which is why I don't understand what has possessed me to agree to meet him here.

"Thanks for coming," he says, reaching for both my hands, as his cheek grazes mine.

And I remember why I agreed to come…to smell his woody aromatic scent again, to feel the electric buzz from his skin holding mine again, to pretend, if only for a few minutes, that the last three years have not happened.

"I can't stay long," I say, pulling my hands from his. "It's past 10pm and I have market runs with my mother tomorrow. Wedding preps, I'm sure you understand."

It is intended as shade, but from the way he smiles at me, it misses its mark.

He nods as we both sit. "I understand." His eyes take me in and his smile widens. "Gosh, you're beautiful, Abi. Even more beautiful than I remember."

I flush and lower my eyes, feeling every resolve I might have had walking into that place crumble like a sandcastle under a heavy wave. He reaches for my hand and squeezes it, making me look up, and I am thrown by the intensity of his gaze.

"I made a mistake, Abi," he says, his eyes holding mine as if in search of something. "I never should have married Bev. You're the one I love. The one I've always loved."

7. KNOCKED UP

Family

Nkoyo & Nosa

"Please add more stew," Nosa says to the burly, tight-faced woman dishing pepper sauce to a bowl of rice. "E get pepper plenty, abi?"

The further tightening of the woman's face communicates she finds the question an insult, and she ignores it. "Which meat you want? Beef or assorted?"

"Only beef. No *shaki* or roundabout, abeg!" Nosa implores, remembering what happened the last time he made the mistake of not clarifying and buying a bowl of assorted meat for Nkoyo. Apparently, the mother of his unborn child has developed apathy towards offal, and he almost had his ears chewed off over that error. Needless to say, it is an error he won't be repeating. "Add plantain, please. The ones on that side. The soft, burnt ones."

After paying for the meal, he dashes across the street to where his car is parked.

"I hope you told them to add extra pepper," Nkoyo says, taking the bowl from him, immediately peeling off its cover and tucking into the spicy meal.

Nosa says nothing, unable to tell her that the *Mama Put* server had been close to pulling him by the ear and walking him out when he'd made that request. Luckily, he doesn't have to, as Nkoyo closes her eyes and moans with pleasure, her craving satisfied. Since discovering the *buka* on their way for their second class, stopping there before every one has become their ritual.

"Has the pregnancy belt been delivered yet?" Nkoyo asks, as they approach the church for their seventh class. She has gotten a kick having her pregnancy gear and baby items delivered to Nosa's new house, a bigger house he just moved into to accommodate her and their child.

He shakes his head, driving into the church compound. "Not yet. Has it been a while you ordered it? Send me the tracking number so I can check its delivery status."

She beams, appreciating his unfailing take-charge attitude, one of the many things she loves about this man. She couldn't have chosen a better father for her child.

THE MARRIAGE CLASS

Remembering her own father's frantic reminder, her eyes widen. "Daddy says Uncle Inyang will be free next weekend, so he'll be flying into town for you both to visit him together."

Nosa nods. "Next weekend is fine. I'll make sure I buy the gift. Uncle Inyang is the one who likes cognac, right?"

"It's Uncle Etete that likes cognac. You're seeing him next. Uncle Inyang likes aged bourbon, twenty years and older."

Nosa nods again as he parks the car. "Got it."

"Adaora was telling me about this clinic in Lekki that offers Lamaze classes," Nkoyo says, as they walk the short distance to the building where their class is to start in less than five minutes. "Remember what we watched on that show on Sunday? Those classes that teach breathing and relaxation techniques to cope with labour?"

"Oh?" is all Nosa can manage in response, jogging his memory to remember what she is talking about.

"Yeah, and it's not expensive either, less than two hundred grand. We should check it out, don't you think?"

He nods for what feels like the thousandth time in the last hour. "Absolutely."

"Family," Ifeyinwa says. "A very loaded word with a million and one meanings and interpretations. But, for the purpose of this journey you are about to begin, it is about two different people coming together to form one unit," her eyes scan the room, "and how your notions of life as single people will change as you assume the role of spouses...and parents."

From the corner of my eye, I see the pregnant woman squeeze her partner's hand and smile at him. For these two, family will mean much more much quicker than it will for the rest of us. I can't help but wonder how one can look forward to something one already has - a pregnancy, in their case - what one isn't sure they want - Raymond - or something once lost that could possibly be gotten back- Lucas.

After Lucas's proclamation at the bar on Friday, I couldn't find any coherent words to say in response, having been completely knocked for six.

"I know it's a lot to dump on you," he'd continued, his eyes wide and imploring.

"And I don't know what you want me to do with it," I'd retorted. "You're married."

In hindsight, I wonder why my being engaged hadn't taken precedence to the reminder of his marital status.

"I know, I know," he had said, rubbing his temple, a habit of his that left me awash with nostalgia, my emotions conflicted, wanting him back so desperately...and hating him for the pain he'd inflicted on me.

"Just sleep on it," he'd said. "Take some time to think about it, and maybe we can talk about it better after you do?"

Nkoyo & Nosa

Nkoyo squeezes Nosa's hand and smiles at him. He smiles back, though not quite as enthusiastically. Even though he has had several months to get used to the idea, the reminder of his impending foray into fatherhood, one he neither planned at this time, nor with this person, is still jarring.

Because never in a thousand years would he have guessed he would end up marrying his junior colleague, Nkoyo.

It was only supposed to be a casual hook up. Still reeling from the breakup with his girlfriend of seven years, Demi, who had left him because she felt 'stifled' and 'suffocated' in their relationship, he had agreed to join his colleagues for drinks at a pub, a monthly ritual he'd never cared to partake in before. Walking into the bar with music so loud his eardrums pulsated, and smoke thick enough to fog up his glasses, as he squeezed his way through the horde of noisy patrons in his search for his colleagues, he was about to turn around to leave after getting accidentally elbowed in the face, when Obinna, a fellow Vice President from the bank, called out his name and beckoned him to the section of the bar where the Hevlos team was seated. Reluctantly, he made his way to join them and, after initially insisting on a glass of tonic water, he'd caved and agreed to have a shot of whisky, one shot that led to several more. As the alcohol loosened him up, his desire to leave ebbed to nothingness, the hitherto intimidating bar now vibrant and exciting, his colleagues' jokes and banter now more engaging and hilarious, the music catchier and more rhythmic. In no time, he was dancing carefree, his dance partners a rotation of his colleagues, male and female, so happy and carefree he could hardly tell one from the other. Until the last person he'd danced with, who, instead of the gyration of hips and limbs of his previous dance partners, had placed soft hands on his chest to steady him when he almost toppled over backwards in his attempt of the *Dakiwe* dance to a popular Amapiano song.

"Take it easy, Nosa."

Against the backdrop of the throbbing beats and deafening music, the soft tone of her voice, soothing and dulcet, was enough to make him stop dancing and take a look - a proper look - at the person he was now dancing with.

Nkoyo's heart skipped a beat when Nosa stopped dancing and looked at her, squinting as if he had never seen her in his life, and not like he hadn't been the one to reach for her when Data, the girl he'd previously been dancing with, was pulled away by Obinna.

"You have a beautiful voice," he said to her. "Has anyone ever told you that?"

Nkoyo laughed, never having heard anything even close. "Really?"

"Really!" he said, moving closer so she could hear him better, but which inadvertently brought their faces into close contact, their foreheads touching.

Taking her hand in his, she put up no resistance when he led her out of the bar, pausing briefly at their table for her to grab her handbag. They had barely gotten to his car when he pulled her closer, cupping her face as his mouth claimed hers in a sloppy kiss. Bespectacled and standing only about five feet and nine inches, he wasn't the kind she typically went for, but that hadn't stopped her from falling for him the first week she'd been hired, as he'd explained the difference between the discounted cash flow and earnings multiplier valuation methods to the class of the bank's new hires, of which she was one. So, that evening, even though she was well aware he was more than a little inebriated, she'd kissed him back. And about thirty minutes later, as they stumbled out of his car and into his bungalow apartment in Oniru, she'd yielded to him. The sex had been intense and he'd displayed more stamina than she'd expected, considering his state of intoxication. He couldn't get enough of her, and she was only too happy to oblige, simultaneous explosive orgasms her reward.

When his eyes opened in the morning, his brows furrowed at the sight of the sleeping form beside him. Squinting, he recognized her from the office, but her name he couldn't for the life of him remember. Hazy images looped in his head, images of them kissing as they entered his apartment, of him popping open her blouse and sending its buttons flying all over the room, of throwing her to his bed and ravaging her all night. Patting his bedside table for his glasses, he rose to his feet when they weren't there, stopping short of stepping on them where they lay by his shoes. He put them on and was about to do the same to his boxer shorts, when he heard her soft moan as she stretched on the bed, the heave of her chest flaunted her large DD breasts, and he felt a familiar stirring. As if sensing his arousal, she sat up in bed, giving him a better view of what looked to be a Brazilian bikini wax.

"You're awake?" she asked, her smile part shy and part coy.

That voice. Her sonorous voice compounded the raging desire rousing within him and, walking to the bed, talking was the last thing he had on his mind. As he made love to her once, twice, several more times that morning, for once, thoughts of Demi were not at the forefront of his mind, the immense sexual gratification enough to make him forget the heartache he nursed, if only for a little while. And as the new week rolled around, he found himself unable to keep his hands off his new lover, Nkoyo, not even when they were at work. For someone who was far from a risk taker and had never broken a rule his whole life, having sex with her in his office was exciting, liberating, and at complete odds with anything he would have dared do in the past, making him feel like a totally different person. When he was with Nkoyo, it was all about the sex, and he was able to pretend that love - and the heartbreak that came with it - didn't exist.

Until Demi called.

THE MARRIAGE CLASS

She'd called him in tears, apologizing profusely for leaving him, telling him all she'd needed was time to clear her head. He agreed to meet her for drinks, and seeing her again made him realize no amount of mind-blowing sex with another woman could trump their deep bond. Without a second thought, he'd ended things with Nkoyo, happy to be back with the true love of his life.

Only to be blindsided by Nkoyo's pregnancy announcement a few weeks later.

"I'm pregnant."

Those two words had hit him like long-range missiles, projectiles he could see coming towards him in slow motion, feeling the deadly impact of each one as they struck, one after the other.

"You're...you're..." was all he could stutter.

"Pregnant, Nosa. Pregnant with your child."

His legs had given way beneath him and he'd collapsed into his chair, unable to say a word in response, looking at her as she glared back at him, daring him to deny responsibility or demand that she 'take care of it', two options he knew were there for him, but neither of which he could take. As the son of a single mother whose father had taken both, he wasn't about to do the same. And as he listened to Nkoyo talk about being six weeks along, and how she was going to have the child regardless of what he said, with a heavy heart, he knew he had to end things with Demi and man up to his responsibility with Nkoyo.

It was only the right thing to do.

As the class breaks up, I am saddened that Raymond didn't show up. Saddened, but, in a very weird sense, relieved. I dial his number, but as it has been doing all weekend, it rings off.

"Your fiancé couldn't make it today?" the pregnant woman asks, as she and her partner walk past where I sit.

"No, he's a bit under the weather," I answer with a strained smile. "He'll be here for the next class."

I am surprised by the certainty and conviction with which I tell this lie because, in truth, I don't know if he will.

On Friday, I didn't leave the bar till well past midnight, driving into my compound at almost 1am…and meeting Raymond leaning on his car in wait. My heart lurched as our eyes made contact, from the surprise I felt over seeing him there and the foreboding I got from his impassive face.

"Wow! What a way to surprise your girl! Have you been waiting long?" I asked, getting out of my car, the smile on my face at odds with the panic – oh, the panic – that was making my insides churn.

"Where are you coming from, Abi?"

"What kind of question is that?" I scoffed. "I told you I was running errands for my mom."

"It's almost 1am, Abi," he stated, his face still devoid of any emotion. "What kind of errands?"

"If you must know, I had to drop some things with my aunties in…in…" I stuttered, my mind blank and chaotic at the same time. "Festac. Yeah, Festac. That's where I'm coming from."

"And, let me guess, there was a lot of traffic, right?" he asked, a clench of his jaw muscles his first facial movement. "At 1am in the morning. Besides, I thought you said you were picking up lace samples from your Aunty Ameze. I didn't know she had moved from Oniru to Festac." He sighed, looking deflated…tired. "What's going on with you, Abi? What's going on with us?"

I opened my mouth, wanting to answer that absolutely nothing was going on with me…or us. But as my eyes held his, my mouth was unable to tell that lie.

Because there was a lot going on with me…with us.

"All the lies, all the excuses this week, all the funny business with your phone…" he sighed again. "These last few weeks have been…off. You've been so distant, here but not really here. We've barely communicated and your mind always seems to be a million miles away." His voice trailed, but his gaze stayed pointed. "It almost feels like…like you don't want to do this."

I knew what *this* meant. I knew exactly what he was asking. But my lips remained immobile, making me unable to say a word.

"Do you still want this?" he asked, directly now. "Do you still want to get married?"

My eyes dropped, and I was unable to hold his gaze, unable to answer his question.

"Abi?" he prodded, the higher lilt of his voice giving away his rising his anxiety, clearly not having expected a less than straightforward answer from me.

I forced myself to look up at him, his eyes wide and desperate, and I bit my lower lip, my heart heavy in my uncertainty.

"I don't know, Raymond. I don't know what I want."

He'd deflated. I watched with dismay as his shoulders slumped and his gaze became unfocused. He looked at me, I knew wanting to hear me recant, to hear me retract my words. But I neither recanted nor retracted. Instead, I bowed my head, not stopping him as he walked past me to his car.

Today, after not calling him all weekend, I shouldn't be surprised he ignored my calls this afternoon, or that he didn't show up tonight. And, walking to my car, I convince myself that this time apart will be good for us.

Because I sure as heck need it more than anything.

THE MARRIAGE CLASS

Nkoyo & Nosa

On the drive home, Nkoyo steals a look at Nosa and sees that he is, as usual, lost in his thoughts. She remembers the time she had his attention, all of it, in the early days of their relationship, when he hadn't been able to keep his eyes and hands off her. She remembers the way he would look at her with hooded eyes that undressed her, regardless of wherever they were. But since the evening she broke the news of her pregnancy, he has not looked at her like that again.

When he'd accepted responsibility for the pregnancy without argument, when he'd broken up with his girlfriend without persuasion, when he'd agreed to her family's demand to marry her immediately without pushback, she hadn't been able to believe her luck. She'd felt victorious, triumphant for snagging for herself a man like him. Smart, sensitive, caring, and financially stable, he was everything she'd prayed for in a husband, and when their families finalized their marriage plans and he presented her with a classy single stone diamond ring, her heart had burst, unable to contain its joy.

But now, four months later, she can't help but feel that everything he has done… is still doing…is simply out of duty.

"What do you think?" he asks about an hour later, as they stand in what will be their son's nursery, eyeing the cloud murals on the wall that have replaced the ghastly animals their decorator initially placed. "I think these are better."

Nkoyo nods and smiles. "Much better. This looks more like a nursery now and less like a zoo." She interlinks her hand with his and winks at him. "We should get her to do mommy and daddy's room as well, something to always set the mood."

His smile is slight and his grip is flaccid. "The rocking chair and ottoman will get here before the weekend, and we can order the brown and blue blanket with matching throw pillows you saw on Amazon. That will complete the room, right?"

As he continues to talk about other possible additions to the room, sounding more like it is a work project than the home he will be sharing with the woman he is to spend the rest of his life with, she is now all too aware that he is not with her out of choice.

8. MR. ARCTIC

Love Languages

"Today's class is all about love languages," Maxwell says, standing before the class. "It is important to be aware not only of one's love language, but, more importantly, your partner's."

His eyes scan the room and land on the attractive middle-aged man, whose attention, as usual, is not on the class but his phone.

"Eric," Maxwell calls out. "Would you like to tell us what yours is?"

Eric looks up at him with a brow raised, more irritated than guilty about being caught not paying attention. "My what?"

"Your love language," Maxwell repeats, crossing his arms, equally defiant.

"Oh, for crying out loud!" Eric chuckles. "The main language I speak is English. A bit of Yoruba if you push, and, if you're lucky, maybe even a little Igbo. But that's it."

There are a few chuckles from the back of the class, but Maxwell's face remains unsmiling.

"I just ran through them, Eric. The five love languages are Words of Affirmation, Acts of Service, Gifts, Quality Time, and Physical Touch. Which would you say is yours?"

Eric shrugs, looking just about as interested as one would watching a kettle of water boil. "Acts of Service, I guess."

"Thank you, Eric," Maxwell says, before turning to Eric's fiancée. "And you, Ivie? What's yours?"

"Hers are all five!" Eric cuts in, laughing. "More than the five, if there are any."

More laughter rings in the class and I notice Ivie looks anything but amused.

"Words of Affirmation," she answers when the laughter dies off, her eyes not straying from Maxwell's face. "That's my love language."

The irony!

As Maxwell directs the question from couple to couple, I look at the empty seat next to me. Raymond and I have not spoken all week, and, looking at the clock, it is already past 7pm, so it is safe to assume he won't attend today's class.

"Abi?"

Maxwell's voice makes my neck snap away from the vacant seat.

"Umm, my love language?" I ask redundantly. "That would be Quality Time."

As Maxwell moves on to the pregnant couple, I can't help but think how varied our different love languages are, with not a single couple in the room having the same one. My eyes veer to Raymond's empty seat again, and I realize that would have been different if he were here. And tears well in my eyes as I think how, sometimes when we find someone willing to speak our language, we often fail to even recognize it.

Ivie & Eric

"What a load of rubbish that was!" Eric chuckles as he and Ivie walk into his house later that night. "As a matter of fact, the entire class is a load of garbage. Those two jokers, Maxwell and his wife, are just reeling off whatever nonsense they can lay their hands on from Google. A complete waste of time."

Ivie's mouth is set in a grim line and she says nothing in response as she kicks off her shoes and pads into the living room, dropping her handbag on the floor, knowing very well that will annoy Eric. And she is correct, as she sees his eyes go first to her shoes at the door then her handbag by the loveseat. She glares at him, daring him to complain or scold her, but, as he senses she is spoiling for a fight, he ignores her shoes and picks up her bag, placing it on the credenza. Sitting on the couch, he switches on the TV and, finding a replay of the UEFA Champions League final match between Liverpool and Real Madrid, he lights a cigar and reclines on the sofa to watch it.

Watching him, Ivie is sorry for her earlier act of defiance and takes a seat next to him on the sofa, tucking her legs under her thighs and placing her head on his shoulder.

But he shrugs her off. "Ivie, please let me watch this game in peace."

He might as well have slapped her across the face.

Pushing herself off, she stands up. "Must you always be so cold about everything? Must you always find a way to suck the joy out of every single thing?"

"Huh?!"

"If I can count on you for anything, it's to be nasty and sarcastic about everything," she continues to rant. "To give a snide retort, you are first on the queue for that. But God forbid you to even display any kind of affection towards me."

THE MARRIAGE CLASS

"Here we go again!" he groans, rubbing his eyes.

"You have been apathetic about this marriage process from the very beginning. If you're not fiddling with your phone in class, you're complaining about the one or two sentences you manage to even hear."

"Don't talk as if you don't know how I feel about this whole thing," he throws back at her, his eyes widening in his rising anger. "Need I remind you that you're the one who gave me a 'marry me, or else' ultimatum. You know very well this is one rodeo I don't care to ride a third time."

This is enough to silence her, and, as they glare at each other, she accepts she has been a fool to expect anything different.

They met three years ago when she worked for an advertising and brand marketing company desperate to secure Eric's company's account. She and her colleagues had gone there to make a presentation, and she had barely been able to concentrate on anything her team mates said, her attention completely stolen by the man at the head of the table, who was listening to them with a raised brow and half smirk playing on his lips, his eyes twinkling with humour. In his early fifties, he was almost two decades older, but age had done little to diminish his rugged good looks, his bushy eyebrows, salt and pepper beard, and long, sloped nose making him look both distinguished and roguish at the same time. Every time he opened his mouth to talk, every time she heard his voice, gravelly and gruff, her body tingled, her eyes unable to peel away from his full lips, her imagination conjuring images of all the possible things those lips could do. From that very first afternoon, she'd known she wanted him.

"Sir, let us run your social media campaign for one month," she said, after the meeting drew to a close and Eric had communicated, in no uncertain terms, that his business would not be moving from the company already handling its social media management and marketing. "A free trial."

From the corner of her eye, Ivie saw her boss, Dotun, turn to glare at her, but she continued, undaunted. "You don't have to pay us anything for a month. If your engagements and, more importantly, sales don't treble by the end of that month, we can simply shake hands and call it a day."

Eric looked at her, his characteristic slow smile forming on his lips as his eyes bored into hers. "Really? A free trial? What's his name here," he tilted his head in Dotun's direction, "looks like he's hearing that for the first time. Isn't that kind of decision way above your pay grade?"

"Not if I pay for it myself," she answered, not breaking gaze. "I'm ready to gamble my one month's salary, and then some, because I'm confident we'll get your business."

"Oh really?" Eric's grin widened. "You're 'confident'?"

"I'm one hundred percent certain," she answered, with a coy smile of her own. "Sir."

He had been immediately fascinated by the brazen young woman and signed them up on the spot. And when

THE MARRIAGE CLASS

engagement on all his company's social media platforms – Facebook, Instagram, Twitter, and LinkedIn – increased by four hundred percent that first month alone, he'd called her.

"I see why you were so 'confident'," had been his opener when she answered her phone.

The sound of his unmistakable voice, and the smile she was certain was on his face, made her melt. She hadn't seen or spoken to him since the pitch meeting, so hearing his voice made her want to levitate.

"We know our job, Sir," she'd answered, her own smile automatic.

"What would it take to get you to stop calling me *Sir*?"

"You simply asking me."

"And getting you to have dinner with me? What would *that* take?"

Her smile broadened and then waned as she remembered her company's strict no-dating-clients policy. "I would have to get another job for that to happen."

"Done. I can get you a meeting with Aphrodite in the morning." Aphrodite was the biggest media and branding company not just in the country, but the entire continent. "Your wish is my command, beautiful Ivie."

She had to purse her lips to stop the giggle from bursting forth from her lips. Even without the assurance of the

Aphrodite meeting happening, or that anything would come out of it if it did, she agreed to dinner with Eric the following evening, and from the moment she walked out of her gate and saw him standing by his chauffeur driven car, dashing in a black, fitted suit and sparkling white shirt unbuttoned enough to reveal a coating of slick, dark hair on his chest, she'd known she would throw everything away for this man.

As they dined at the Korean restaurant he'd chosen, he found himself even more taken by her, her quick wit matching his, something that was not at all an easy feat. Even though he had initially intended his dalliance with her to be brief, not going beyond a few dates and a few rolls in the hay, as they talked and laughed over their meal of *japchae* and *bulgogi*, he knew he wanted to see a whole lot more of her. And kissing her goodnight as he dropped her at home, he had been just as aroused by the feel of her luscious lips and silky smooth skin as he was by the wide-eyed look of admiration in her eyes. He could tell she fancied him, wanted him - not his money, but *him* - and that was a turn on more than any other thing.

Luckily, the meeting with Aphrodite went well, but long before she resumed as their Client Relationship Vice President for the West African region, she and Eric had become a thing, a bona fide couple. And, for both of them, it was just as wonderful, just as explosive, just as amazing as they'd fantasized.

For a while.

THE MARRIAGE CLASS

By the end of their first year together, as much as she still enjoyed his jokes, bants, and quips, she found herself increasingly making excuses for why his display of affection was only confined to the bedroom in their throes of passion. She found herself excusing the fact that, outside of that, there were no terms of endearment, no hugs, no kisses, nothing that would differentiate them from business associates enjoying a night out. She explained away his abhorrence of any form of public display of affection, justified why he never wanted her to sleep over why he almost always insisted on sending her home, no matter how late it was, and how he would sometimes go days without as much as sending her a text message, telling herself his prior marriages had left him badly burned...badly scarred.

But now, as their eyes hold in his living room, she can't help but wonder if they were doomed from the very start.

9. COMPATIBLE...NOT

Conflict Management

Ogechi & Zulu

"Bia, this woman, class has already started! Where are you nau? Must I always get here before you? This your behavior is very abominable!"

Ogechi rolls her eyes as she listens to the voice note, seated in her car. "No be only *abdominable*," she mocks his pronunciation of the word. "Abdomen *nko*."

Switching off her car, she exhales and raps her long fingernails on her steering wheel, trying to muster the zeal to get out of the car and head to the building in front of her, for their ninth class, her anxiety over their fast approaching wedding making her want to break out in

THE MARRIAGE CLASS

hives. Exhaling again, she grabs her bag, opens the door, and swings her legs out of the car. Best to get tonight's class over and done with.

Walking into the class, with his bright yellow t-shirt, it isn't difficult to spot Zulu. Why he insists on only wearing loud, garish colours for clothing is something she will never understand. Their eyes meet and from the narrowing of his, he is not pleased she is late yet again.

If only he knows he should be happy she's there at all!

He grunts as she takes a seat and she mumbles a greeting back, not bothering with any apologies or excuses. She's there, and that's what's important.

"Conflict Management is one of the most important skills to have, period. Not just in marriage," Ifeyinwa says to the class. "*However*, in a marriage, it is extremely important for each party to be aware of all triggers - theirs *and* their partner's."

As she talks, I see that most people are either listening keenly or scribbling away furiously, engaged by the day's subject. I, on the other hand, am unable to comport myself well enough to listen, let alone take any notes. I look, again at the empty seat next to mine. For the third class in a row, Raymond hasn't shown up, but the bigger tragedy is that I haven't seen or spoken to him in over a week, not since the confrontation in front of my house. My calls have gone unanswered and I have not been brave enough to go looking for him at home or work, afraid of what he will say…or what I will say…what I will own up to.

Because I met up with Lucas again.

This past weekend, he requested we meet at a more private restaurant, and we spent Saturday evening reminiscing about the good times we had in the past. Like our first meeting, we were there till past midnight, and when he walked me to my car, he tried to kiss me. As tempted as I was to let him, I pushed him away, not quite ready to go that far that quickly. But I agreed to meet him at Abel's bachelor pad the next day.

Abel is his best friend and former flat mate.

Even as I did, I knew it was a very dangerous move.

"I've missed you, Abi. I've missed you so much," Lucas said, as we sat on the couch in Abel's living room, his friend having conveniently vacated the house to 'run errands'. "I want you so much."

He was so close to me, I could feel his breath on my neck, and as his hand went on my thigh and his nose brushed my cheek, even though I knew what was coming next, even though everything in me screamed *run*, I sat there as he tilted my face to his, and as his lips took mine. My unruly hands went to his face and held it, deepening the kiss, relishing the familiarity that was the feel of his lips and the way his tongue swished in my mouth, both in duet and combat with mine. But as one of his hands cupped my breast and the one on my thigh pushed higher up in the direction of my throbbing lady parts, I knew it was time to jump out of that fiery, hot furnace.

"I have to go," I managed to say, pushing him away.

"Abi, please don't do this," he said, his arousal making his already deep voice deeper still, thick in its need to relive the intense passion we'd shared in years past. "If you don't want me, why have you been coming to meet me?" he asked, and with very good reason. "Stop fighting your feelings, Abi. You want this just as badly as I do."

"I have to go," I repeated, doing everything to drown out his words, to keep his words from rendering to naught any self-control I had.

Scrambling to my feet with whatever shavings of dignity I still held, I walked as fast as I could to the door, grateful for the back-of-the-hand knowledge I still had of the house that had once been his, knowing how to open the stiff lock and let myself out before he could stop me.

Now, as Ifeyinwa talks, I scroll through the messages from Lucas that he has sent me today, different variants of what he has already told me; that he is still madly in love with me, that he wants to leave his wife, that he wants me to leave Raymond. And all I can think is how quickly conflict can switch from a good thing…to a bad thing.

A very bad thing.

ADESUWA O'MAN NWOKEDI

Ogechi & Zulu

Ogechi's eyes narrow into slits when Zulu finally walks into the studio the following afternoon. Not only is he late for their pre-wedding photo shoot, in a white suit over a black turtleneck, he couldn't be more deviated from what she had asked - make that *pleaded* - he wear. As their eyes meet, from the hard set of his, she can see that neither was a mistake; neither his being late nor his choice of attire. He has done both to provoke her.

"But you were supposed to wear a black suit and a white shirt," Ogechi retorts, unable to mask her anger…and disgust. "What is this thing you are wearing?"

"You said black and white," Zulu answers, waving in greeting at Ade, the photographer. "This is black and white."

Ogechi's nostrils flare and she fights back the tears that are threatening to rush forth from her eyes, feeling like, finally, he has pushed her to the wall. She avoids making eye contact with her makeup artist and stylist, both of whom, she is certain, are in disbelief seeing the man she is set to marry. In a turtleneck made from fabric so shiny, it looks like a whole can of glitter has been emptied on it, and a white suit with the kind of pointy lapels that stopped being fashionable in the nineties, Zulu paints the picture of the very kind of man she is desperate for him not to. After he refused her offer to get him a stylist for the shoot, she'd sent him the link for a sleek Mai Atafo suit, convinced he couldn't go wrong with that. But, as it appears, her offer for a stylist was not the only thing he declined. With this being the first of their three planned photo shoots, the others scheduled for later that month at the beach, she is now mortified about how all three sets of pictures will turn out.

"But I thought you said he was wearing a Mai suit," her stylist, Sadiq, remarks, his bewilderment evident in his stage whisper.

And this is enough to release the reins she has struggled to keep her tongue in.

"What kind of Aba looking suit is this?" she explodes at Zulu, quivering in her unleashed rage. "Do you know how ridiculous you look?" She turns to Sadiq and Natufe, her makeup artist. "Can you imagine what he actually chose to wear? Can you imagine what he wants to wear standing next to me? After all the hassle we went through to get this dress, he shows up here looking like a local Igbo man!"

In an elaborate white corset dress with a bishop collar stoned in black onyx stones from the yet to be released line of one of the country's biggest designers, Madonna Isa, a dress Ogechi for which had to pay an almost seven-figure amount as the designer refused to loan it to Sadiq, the trouble her team has gone through for her to be properly attired is evident.

The smile on Zulu's face disappears, her words pelting him like the bullets she has intended. "A local Igbo man, Ogechi?" he repeats. "What should I look like before? An English man? A Yoruba man?" He nods in Sadiq's direction. "Or a confused man, like this one?"

In patchwork denim dungarees worn over a black mid-riff tank top, Sadiq squirms, his light skin almost matching his bright red hair and fingernails. "Let's give them some privacy," he says to Natufe, before sashaying out of the room with his head bowed. Ade follows the pair out of the studio.

"Did you have to resort to insults?" Ogechi snaps.

"Oh, you're the only one who has the authority to insult, *abi*?" Zulu demands. "*Bia*, what is wrong with looking like an Igbo man, Ogechi? This is not the first time you will make that kind of statement."

"I sent you the link for a suit, a proper suit!" she cuts in, waving her hands in her exasperation. "All you had to do was buy that one. That was all I asked of you, Zulu!"

In truth, it was something he could have easily done. But something about her message had riled him enough to immediately disregard it.

This suit will work for the shoot. It's a bit pricey but it will give you the right look. Just send them a DM to order, had been her condescending message on the Instagram app he hardly used.

THE MARRIAGE CLASS

Work for the shoot. The right look. Those phrases grated, the implication that none of his clothing would *work for the shoot* or give him *the right look* not lost on him. In rebellion, he'd deleted the message and ordered a suit from a Port Harcourt based designer – a very expensive designer, for that matter – he favoured. And even though he hadn't gone with Ogechi's preferred choice of outfit, he'd left home that day confident he was well turned out for their photo shoot. But everything from the disdainful look on her face when she saw him, to the caustic words she had just thrown at him, to her wide-eyed agitation as she now glared at him, had not only punctured his confidence, confidence he found increasingly delicate when he was with her, it had deflated it outright.

"I don't know how a man can be so stubborn!" Ogechi was still ranting. "Every time I try to correct you when it comes to your dressing, your grammar, the way you chew with your mouth open for the whole world to make out all the ingredients of your food, all I get from you is push back. Are you determined to be uncouth for the rest of your life?"

"That's good, you are finally speaking your mind," Zulu answers, nodding as if in sudden comprehension. "You are finally saying the things that have been swallowing your stomach since we met."

Ogechi hisses and shakes her head. "Instead of you to listen when someone is trying to help you…"

"I don't need your help, Ogechi!" he explodes, his rage now matching hers. "I am a forty-one year old man and I am not about to change for anybody. What you see now is what you will get forever."

She recoils, taken aback as he has never raised his voice at her before.

"Listen, Ogechi," he says, after a few minutes of uncomfortable silence. "If you despise everything from the way I dress, to the way I talk, to the way I eat…why did you agree to marry me?"

As their eyes hold, it is a question she is unable to answer.

A few months before, a mutual friend, Chinasa, introduced them. A thirty-eight year old career-minded investment banker, Ogechi was known for her very cynical views on relationships and men. Highly intellectual, slightly neurotic, and with a textbook Type-A personality, none of her previous relationships had progressed beyond a few months. It also didn't help that she had an inflexible list of criteria any man she would date needed to satisfy. But with age forty only a few years away, she'd decided to relax this list – in truth, more like shred it – when she agreed to not just date but marry the less intelligent and, in her opinion, very uncivilized Zulu.

For Zulu, she had mesmerized him from the first evening they met for dinner. He had stared at her with wide-eyed fascination, captivated by the way she spoke, the way she enunciated her every word, hypnotized by her large eyes and how they appeared even larger as she spoke, charmed by the shallow dimples that dipped into her fluffy cheeks. And, walking her to her car, spellbound by her wide hips that perfectly matched her full bosom. Full bodied and voluptuous, she ticked all his boxes and he couldn't believe his luck that such a gorgeous, intelligent, sophisticated woman was not only single, but had agreed to date him. So enchanted was he that, even as he noticed, over time, how argumentative and stubborn she could be, traits he'd never believed he could tolerate in a partner, he was quick to discount them, choosing to instead focus on the things about her he did love.

Alas, she hadn't accorded him the same favour.

"Hi, guys. I'm sorry to interrupt, but we're already thirty minutes into your time slot," Ade says, peering through the door. "I have another shoot at 4pm."

Wordlessly, Ogechi and Zulu take position next to each other, plastering smiles on their faces and holding hands at Ade's prompt. When they are made to stand facing each other, Zulu's hands on her waist and hers on his shoulders, as their eyes lock, their mutual resentment is evident and their phony wide smiles are unable to mask it.

After what has got to be the most laborious fifty minutes of all their lives, Ade's inclusive, the session finally comes to an end.

"I'll send them to you so you can pick the best ones for editing," Ade says, scrolling through the images on his camera. He shrugs, his dissatisfaction with the outcome evident. "I'll make these work somehow. But guys, better energy for the next shoot, please!"

Optimistic thinking on his part, that there will be a 'next shoot'.

"I hope you didn't drive here," Zulu says, after Ogechi has changed into the jeans and tank top she wore to the studio, and is gathering her things into bags. "Remember I asked you not to."

"I didn't drive here, Zulu," she snaps, wishing she'd ignored his request and *had* driven herself there.

"*Nwuye'm*, I'm sorry about wearing what you don't like," Zulu says on the ride home, covering her hand with his. "I promise to wear whatever you ask me to for the next shoot."

Ogechi says nothing in response and just stares ahead. She catches his driver's eyes in the rearview mirror and wonders why they must always have audience in the car. With the way Zulu demanded she not drive that day, one would have thought he wanted them to spend quality time together on the drive home…alone.

"Let's go somewhere nice to eat," Zulu says, oblivious of her irritation. "Anywhere of your choice."

Not in this your white suit, she thinks to herself, throwing him a scathing look. In what he is wearing, she will not be caught dead anywhere with him. Before she can say anything in response, her phone rings. It is Shina, her boss.

"Hi, Shina. I'm good, thank you. No, I'm not busy," she answers, fishing in her bag for a notepad and pen.

THE MARRIAGE CLASS

Zulu frowns, angered over how she has discounted his presence to nothing. She is not busy indeed. He watches as she nods, grunts, and writes in her notepad, interjecting here and there, and laughing several times. But it is her closing remark that unleashes the fire of Hades in his belly.

"Not a problem. I'll be at the office tomorrow to tidy up the proposal. You'll get it by lunch time."

"You'll be where which tomorrow?" Zulu asks, when she is off the call. "Isn't tomorrow a Sunday?"

She shrugs, the look on her face baffled. "So?"

Oh, she has got to be kidding him!

"*Bia*, I hope you're not going to make a habit of going to work on Sundays after we're married, Oge," he scoffs. "Even Saturdays are a big no. So, you better let your people know."

She cocks her head to the side in her disbelief. Oh, he has got to be kidding her!

"Are you having a laugh or something? Do you think I got where I am by turning down work? By telling my employers I'm unavailable at any time? Zulu, if I haven't already made it clear, my work is important to me, and it will remain so after we are married. So, whenever my bosses snap their fingers for me to jump, best be certain I'll be asking them how high."

Zulu's jaw clenches. "Well, I will not allow it. If it means us looking for a less demanding job for you, then that's what we will have to do. As you know, I am more than capable of taking care of you and all your expensive needs."

Ogechi bursts into mirthless laughter, clapping her hands as she does, not even caring about the third set of ears, or eyes, in the car. "This guy, you're a joker oh! Less demanding what? You must out of your mind to say something that ridiculous."

"Woman, you better watch your tongue!"

"Woman, indeed!" she continues to cackle. But as quickly as the laughter came, it fades and she glares at him. "Never you try that in your life, Chizulukeme. In your whole life, never you make such a stupid demand of me. Quit my job for what? For whom? Please, never say that kind of thing again."

"Or what? Or what will happen?" Zulu demands, his calm voice belying the inferno raging within him. "Be careful, Ogechi. In your better interest, I will advise you not call my bluff."

10. MAYBE EVER AFTER

Past, Present, Future

Omasan & Itse

It was the year 2003, and they fell in love hard.

They were in their first year of medical school at the University of Lagos, the one year spent at the Akoka campus before proceeding to the College of Medicine at Idi-Araba. He had been standing behind her in the lecture theatre for their Chemistry 101 class, packed with all the first year science and engineering students, and more than a few carry-over students from other years. Someone had pushed past him, making him lose his balance and fall forwards. Her back had broken his fall, and she had turned to glare at him. But in a meet-cute that would have been perfect for the best of romantic movies, their eyes held and everything – her irritation and his anger with the person who'd pushed him – faded to oblivion.

"Are you okay?" she'd mouthed instead.

He'd smiled, nodded, and gave her the thumbs up sign, because he had been too enraptured by her face, her heart-shaped face and tilted eyes that almost looked East Asian, to even manage a word, let alone a sentence in response.

On her part, she'd noticed him before that first meeting; the six-footer with an afro that lent him even more height, who appeared to prefer the company of his headphones to human interaction. So, even though she had turned around with the intention to insult whomever had dared shove her, she'd been stunned to see him - the tall guy - star struck by how even better looking he looked up close, her distant admiration not having allowed her properly appreciate his sleepy eyes and full lips. Turning back to the class, she had been unable to concentrate on anything else, her mind on the guy standing behind her, worried about how she looked from behind and if her love handles were visible in the fitted bodysuit she wore over her jeans. If only she knew he hadn't seen any love handles, but had instead been unable to peel his eyes away from her bum, small and narrow, reminding him of Kylie Minogue's in her infamous *Spinning Around* music video – pert, perky, perfect.

He'd waited for her after class, they had exchanged names and she'd given him her room number. In no desire to play it cool, he'd gone to visit her in her C-block Moremi Hall room that same evening, and they had talked until the

THE MARRIAGE CLASS

10pm curfew for male visitors. She had walked him out of her hostel to the gate of his, Jaja Hall, and they'd talked outside until 2am.

And they were inseparable after that.

Theirs was the relationship everyone modeled theirs after, friends and strangers alike. They were the perfect couple, the perfect team. Years later, during their housemanship year, they moved in together, first to the small room Itse was assigned within the hospital's premises, and then to a mini flat they found in Idi-Araba. After school, as Itse moved to the General Hospital and as Omasan was hired, first by a private hospital in Surulere and later by a highbrow specialist hospital in Victoria Island, they moved to a bigger apartment in Yaba. So tight a unit were they, most of their friends and family considered them married.

Except, of course, they weren't.

"It is extremely important to build a solid foundation in any relationship, especially a marriage," Maxwell says, pacing in front of the class. "It is very important to determine your 'why'." Turning to the class, he nods in the direction of the couple seated at the back of the class. "What is your why, Itse?"

Itse shrugs, his face impassive. "What do you mean?"

"What is your 'why' to get married?" Maxwell repeats. "Why are you taking this very important step?"

Itse shrugs again. "Because everyone around us seems to think getting married is the right thing to do."

My brows shoot up, surprised by his bluntness. If the look on Maxwell's face is anything to go by, so is he.

"Care to elaborate?" Maxwell prods.

Itse leans forward, obviously passionate about the topic. "This whole concept of marriage is ridiculous to me. Why does society demand the validation that comes from a ring on the finger and signature on a piece of paper, over and above every other thing? Who says commitment has to be defined solely by swearing some oath and feeding a thousand mouths after a useless ceremony? Who says I can't be a hundred percent committed to my partner just by telling her I am?"

"Umm," Maxwell stutters, struggling to answer Itse's questions. "It's not a baseless oath but a promise before God and man that validates a couple's commitment to each other."

My brows furrow, my lips twist, and I fold my arms, wishing Maxwell had come up with a more convincing response. Turning to look at Itse as he sits back in his chair, the smile on his face is the confirmation he knows he has the stronger argument tonight. Thankfully, the rest of us are too convinced about why we are here to change our minds at that point.

Well, almost all of us.

With Raymond absent for yet another class, I know I'm going to have to find a way, any way, to reach him. Because it is no longer funny.

Omasan & Itse

"What the hell was that, Itse?" Omasan yells as their car pulls out of the church premises. "What kind of display was that? Why did you embarrass me like that?"

"I didn't embarrass you. I just answered the question the man asked," Itse says through grit teeth. "Or should I have lied?"

"Are you as unwilling to get married as you expressed in there?" Omasan demands. "Is that how you really feel?"

"But why are you acting like you don't know this?" he exclaimed. "You know where I stand when it comes to marriage. You know we're only engaged because you made that a condition for us getting back together." He turns to look at her. "Baby, there is absolutely nothing wrong with the way we are now. We don't need a piece of paper to legitimize our relationship."

"Except I do, Itse!" she shouts, her vocal chords straining. "*I* do!"

You are the love of my life, Abi. I never should have let you go.

Lucas's last text message replays in my head as I make the solo drive back to the island after class. I have lost count of the text messages he has sent me in the week it has been since I last saw him at Abel's place; all of them pleading, all of them cajoling, all of them persuading me to give him another chance.

I remember the happier times we had in our relationship. Full of life and charming, being with Lucas was fun…exciting…passionate. But, if I'm to be honest, it wasn't like that all the time; fun…exciting…nor passionate.

It is so easy to look back on the past through rose-tinted glasses.

As many as there were good times, there were bad times, times I had to deal with his volatile mood swings, times he would flare up for no reason, times he would be incommunicado for days, leaving me hanging and on edge. In hindsight, I realize half of the excitement from being with him came from the nerves and anxiety, the agitation over not knowing which Lucas I would get on any given day, of not knowing if he would be loving or distant, of wondering why he had behaved a certain way, of worrying as I dissected my every word and every action for anything that could have been a trigger. And when he would come out of his foul moods and choose to shower me with affection, my anxiety would give way to elation.

So, yes, there was always excitement, but no, not always the good kind.

And then, in the last few months of our relationship, his constant need for 'space'.

"You're crowding me, Abi. You're crowding me!" was what he said most times I pressed for us to spend more time together, or when I demanded an explanation for the strange phone calls he was all of a sudden receiving.

In those last few weeks, his moodiness was more constant than intermittent, and I was anxious more times than I was elated, but I held on to the frayed rope of that relationship like it was a lifeline, like it was the only thing capable of keeping me alive. So, that Sunday night when he finally severed that rope, telling me it was best for us to go our separate ways, without that lifeline, I was set adrift in the deep blue sea, and when I saw his banns of marriage mere weeks later…I sank.

Until I met Raymond.

Last night, I picked up an *Archie and Veronica* comic that had been on my coffee table for weeks, or at least I'd thought it was an *Archie and Veronica* comic. Raymond gave it to me weeks ago, but I hadn't even bothered opening it, tossing it on my coffee table and forgetting about it thereafter. It wasn't until last night that I saw it wasn't an *Archie and Veronica* comic after all, but one customized for us, with characters named *Raymond and Abi*.

To the love of my life, Abi! Of all the love stories out there, ours is my favourite one, Raymond had written on the dedication page. The realization that he had created the comic for me...for us...melted my heart.

A lump rises in my throat and tears blind my eyes as I navigate my car down Osborne Road, realizing how nostalgia can oftentimes colour the reality of the past, making it difficult to enjoy the present.

And messing up all good for a future.

11. COLD FEET

For Better, For Worse

"The truth is, this journey you're about to embark on, this journey called marriage," Ifeyinwa says in our final class, "is just as much for better…as it is for worse."

Her eyes move from one person to the next, from one couple to the next, and I see the furrow in her brows when they rest on me…and the empty chair beside me. Thankfully, her eyes continue their scan of the room. With a number of empty seats, there are a few other couples absent.

"As the years go by, there will be times you'll ask yourself why it's so hard, times you'll feel like you're giving more than you are taking, times you'll want everything to change but nothing does, times you'll be resentful about not putting yourself first." She stops for emphasis. "In any long term relationship, these feelings are inevitable, and nothing Maxwell and I can say in this class can subvert them. But what we will leave you with is this piece of advice; don't let them fester, don't wait too long to talk about them or, very importantly, get support. Remember that, like you, your partner is an imperfect being, so expecting perfection will only set your marriage up for disaster. Rather, learn how to celebrate this imperfect love. Don't sweat the small stuff, nurture each other, and remain focused on the things you *do* love about this human being you have committed forever to. That's the only way that for better or worse can be possible."

After the class, I am the first person headed to the door, in my haste to catch Raymond at home, knowing there is absolutely no way he will turn me away if I'm right there at his door. With our August 27th wedding date just two months away, our mothers are on the phone daily, finalizing plans for the ceremonies, both of them happening in Benin. I have a final fitting for my wedding and reception gowns next week, and my childhood friend and maid-of-honour, Esosa, has finally confirmed her flight from London after an initial scare of not getting time off work. That the impending bride and groom have not communicated in two weeks is an atrocity.

"Abi, please wait," Ifeyinwa calls out.

I tense hearing my name and turn around, allowing the other people in class file past me. A few of them, Ewa and Chioma, hold my eyes with theirs, and my stomach drops when I recognize the pity in theirs. It is no mystery what

THE MARRIAGE CLASS

Ifeyinwa wants to talk to me about. Everyone knows my fiancé has been a no-show for several classes.

"Is everything okay?" Ifeyinwa asks. "You've been alone for a couple of weeks. Is Raymond okay? Is he out of town?"

"Umm," I don't know whether to lie or just blurt out the truth. I choose the former. "Umm, yeah. He's had some work commitments."

"I see," Maxwell says from where he is leaning on a table, cross armed. His brows are knotted and it is obvious he doesn't buy my answer. "When did you say your wedding is?"

"August 27th."

Ifeyinwa and Maxwell exchange a glance, before returning their attention to me.

"You know what? Give us a call when Raymond is back, and Maxwell and I will be happy to cover the topics he missed, in a single class just for the two of you," Ifeyinwa says, with forced cheer. "Does that work?"

"Yes, it does," I nod, lightheaded with relief. "Thank you. We'll call you later this week to schedule it. Thank you so much."

Walking out of the class, I am comforted, grateful not only for the chance to repeat the classes with Raymond, but also for the opportunity to be doing it with him - the classes...and forever. Because if there is one thing the last few weeks have shown me, it is that Raymond is the one, the only one, I want to spend forever with.

Abi & Raymond

My heart is pounding as I wait, not wanting to ring the doorbell a second time. The guards in Raymond's apartment complex let me into the premises without question – less from cognizance and more because of the generous tips I give them - and his car in the garage is confirmation that he is home. I am steeling myself to ring the bell again, when the door opens. My breath catches in my throat at the first sight of Raymond in weeks, and even though his face is leaner, his beard fuller, and his eyes more sunken than I have ever seen them, my heartbeat accelerates, confirmation that, over and above anyone else, he is the one I love.

"What do you want?" he asks, his voice flat, his face taut.

My shoulders slump, disappointed by his cold reception, gutted he hasn't pulled me into his arms, gushing about how much he has missed me.

"I get it, Raymond. I get it. I messed up and you wanted to punish me," I answer, smiling at him. "These last two weeks have been hell and I've missed you."

THE MARRIAGE CLASS

His eyes narrow and he leans on the doorpost, blocking my way as I try to walk in.

"I'm asking again what you want, Abi."

"What kind of question is that? And why don't you want me to come in? Or is there someone inside?" I bristle at the mere thought. "Raymond Ogieni, do you have another woman in there?"

"Not all of us are two-timing liars like you, Abi," he scoffs, his eyes narrowing. "I know you've been meeting up with your ex."

"My...my ex?" I repeat inanely, feeling like buckets of ice cold and scalding hot water have been upturned over me, both at the same time.

"Lucas Ibazebo, that's his name, isn't it? I hear you two have been meeting up at his friend's house in Oniru for your trysts," Raymond says, before shaking his head and laughing, the most mirthless laugh in the history of laughter. "I've finally accepted the bitter truth that I have only been a filler for you, and that he's the one you've wanted all this time."

"Which trysts? That's a lie!" I exclaim, not having the courage to admit meeting Lucas at Abel's place, even if only once.

"Abel Asukwo's brother happens to be a friend of mine. I bet you didn't know that."

I sigh, cornered. "I met up with Lucas there only once..."

"Say no more. I don't need the gory details," Raymond says, dropping his eyes, as if he can no longer stand the sight of me. "All the sneaking around, the addiction to your phone…it was all him, wasn't it? I was a fool to think you'd be ready to start over with me." He shakes his head. "We're done."

"What do you mean, done?" I demand, my voice rising in my frustration. I grab him by the arm, my eyes widening at the implication of what he has just said. "When our wedding is less than two months away? When everything is already set? Are you out of your mind, Raymond?"

He looks at me and there is a visible clench to his jaw. "What's more important to you, Abi? The wedding…or a marriage?" He shrugs. "You've made it crystal clear you'd rather be in a nasty entanglement with her *married* ex."

I stand there, too stunned to even articulate anything sensible in response.

How did we get here?

After the breakup with Lucas in February 2020, seeing his banns of marriage in the church bulletin less than two months later had led to something akin to a nervous breakdown for me. I'd slumped on the pew and it had taken my sister, Joyce, sprinkling on my face water from a nursing mother's flask to revive me. But even though I'd risen to my feet and walked out of the church unaided, even though I'd put on the appearance of being fine, something inside me died that day. I got home and proceeded to call Lucas, once, twice, a hundred times, but if the constant busy signal was any indicator, he had blocked my number. But not even that realization made me relent, and I soon took to calling him from anyone's phone I could lay my hands on. He went on to block the numbers of all my family members as well, so I was soon harassing our domestic staff, our security guards, my work colleagues, heck, even strangers, for their phones. When Lucas answered calls from these unfamiliar numbers, upon hearing my voice, he would terminate the calls...every single time.

I think that was when my parents and sister saw that I was spiraling...unraveling. They'd staged an intervention, pleading with me to forget about Lucas and move on, but not even them confiscating my phone had been enough to rid me of the obsession to talk to him, to convince him I was the one he should marry, and not the twenty-five-year-old Beverly whom I was sure was an airhead, an airhead that could never love him the way I did. It wasn't until my sister found pictures of his wedding that I accepted there was no turning back, and that he had left me for real.

"Their wedding was in Jos. He's been telling people he had to get married that far away from Lagos to keep you from showing up and scattering the place," Joyce said, sounding both infuriated and dead tired of the whole thing. "Forget the guy, Abi. There are better men out there."

That was the turning point for me. That was when I decided to move on. But even though I did 'move on', and was finally able to overcome my obsession to see him, for the next few months, I was a walking zombie, barely able to function. I operated in autopilot mode, in a miserable, monotonic existence, going nowhere apart from work, avoiding church like the plague, lest I was accosted with unwanted information about Lucas and his new bride, Beverly. But, by Christmas, eight months after seeing that blasted church bulletin, and seven months after his wedding, I decided to make some radical changes, moving out of my parents' Ikeja GRA home to a mini-flat in Lekki Phase 1, the reminder that I would be turning thirty-two years old the following year all the motivation I needed to box all memories of my former love and open myself to new relationship opportunities. After speaking on the phone with several guys my friends thought I would 'click with', with none of whom I actually did, I agreed to my cousin's suggestion to meet an old friend of hers on a blind date.

Walking into the restaurant, Ricardo's, that evening and seeing the bearded man waving me over, I was relieved he wasn't awful looking. And my sentiments were echoed as I took my seat.

"I'm sorry if I'm staring, but you're gorgeous," Raymond said, grinning from ear to ear. "I almost didn't agree to meet this cousin of Usiomo's she's been raving so much about, not knowing how I would politely tell her I wasn't interested." He shook his head as if in amazement. "But, am I glad I came!"

Seeing his enthusiasm and unmasked enchantment buoyed me, the assurance that I was still attractive to a good man everything I didn't even know I needed. We'd talked for hours and I'd laughed, *really* laughed, for the first time in almost a year. By the end of that date, I knew seeing him again would not be a bad idea at all. Thankfully, he wanted the same thing, and we met up for drinks after work the next day.

"I honestly didn't think I could ever click with anyone again after what I recently went through," I confided in him, as we nursed our cocktails.

"Usiomo told me," Raymond answered. "I promise not to rush you. If you think I'm going too fast, just let me know, and I'll step on the breaks." He paused before continuing. "I really like you, Abi. I know you might not be ready now, but, if it's alright with you, I'd like to hang around until you are."

That was the moment, the very moment, he'd won my heart, and by the end of that week, we'd shared our first kiss. Caring, doting, and attentive, Raymond was the perfect panacea for everything I had suffered in the past year. He was God-sent and falling for him had been a no-brainer.

Until March 2022, a year into our relationship and a few days before the surprise birthday party I'd planned for him, when, while clearing my room, I stumbled on a box where I'd packed up all memories of Lucas; cards, pictures, letters, everything. I sat in my room that afternoon, poring through the memorabilia one by one, remembering happy times with the man I had loved with an all-consuming intensity, and I soon found myself sucked into a labyrinth of nostalgia…and longing. That was when Lucas became the third party in what had started off a beautiful and perfect relationship between Raymond and I. That was when I started comparing everything Raymond said or didn't say, did or didn't do, with Lucas...and Raymond came short all the time. Even with his proposal a few days later. While Lucas's had been intimate and intense, Raymond's was fortuitous and charmless...or at least, that was what I told myself it was.

But now, standing there before him, Raymond is neither charmless nor fortuitous. In stark clarity, I can now see that he is the man with whom my heart is at rest. Not Lucas.

Never Lucas.

"Baby, please," I plead, stepping closer so that a mere breath now separates us. "I haven't behaved well and I'm sorry. It will never happen again, I promise you. I swear to you that I will never set my eyes on Lucas ever again." My voice breaks as tears pool in my eyes. "Please, Raymond. I love you. I love you so much. *You're* the one I want, and not a big, society wedding. All you have to do is say the word, and I'll elope with you to Ikoyi Registry tomorrow." I laugh and wipe the tears from my eyes. "Or even tonight, if we can find someone willing to marry us."

He doesn't even crack a smile, and the hardness in his eyes makes my stomach sink.

"We're done, Abi. I can never trust you again."

12. I DO, I DON'T

Decisions

Bianca & Prince

Disembarking the *danfo* at Masha bus stop, Bianca heaves a sigh of relief to have gotten home in one piece. Not one for public transport, especially since she started dating Prince two years ago, with their relationship now hanging in the balance, she has been less inclined to spend a fortune transporting herself to Yaba for marriage class.

She squints as the light from an overhead streetlight shines on her face. Today was the last class and she is just as clueless about when, or if, she and Prince will get married. In the weeks it has been since their argument, that *if* has gone from lowercase to all uppercase, the likelihood that their relationship will ever translate from her wearing an engagement ring on her finger to them exchanging vows before an altar diminishing by the day. Since their argument, they have gone from speaking several times a day to now going several days without a call from either party. He, disappointed by her accusation of him having a family in Canada, and her, exhausted by it all.

Turning into her street, she stops at a kiosk to buy lozenges to forestall a cough she can feel gathering momentum deep in her chest, not ready to add a cold to her laundry list of problems. Rather than waste time dreaming about and planning for a wedding that will never be, she might as well get more serious about looking for a job.

"Na three hundred naira. You neva pay me for the one you buy for morning," Isa, the owner of the kiosk, says in his nasal voice. "Or you fit give me tomorrow, no problem."

She opens her wallet and, having used all her small change to pay for the bus ride home, is wondering whether to break the one thousand naira notes she has or take Isa up on his offer to pay later, when she notices a figure leaning on the long-abandoned Peugeot 505 car parked in front of her parents' compound. Handing Isa a one-thousand-naira note, without waiting for change, she starts walking towards her building, her brows furrowed and her eyes on the strange man in front of her house that late in the evening. As she approaches, the man turns.

And her heart leaps into her mouth.

"Prince?" she gasps, the bag of sweets dropping to the floor as her hands fly to her face.

THE MARRIAGE CLASS

Standing in front of her, in a black short-sleeved shirt over a pair of jeans, with the same broad smile he wears in the pictures she has taped to her mirror, and not the scowl he has worn in their more recent video calls, is the man whose voice and personality she fell in love with. The same man now standing before her in the flesh.

"Biancaaaah," he grins. "You're even more beautiful in person."

That is enough to unglue her feet from where she has stood rooted, and she rushes forward, leaping into his arms, wrapping hers around his neck in a fierce embrace, holding him tight lest he be a mirage set to disappear in seconds, determined never to let him go. She inhales deeply and smiles as they detach, desperate for a better, closer look at him.

"You smell like lavender and mint," she remarks, cradling his face, her smile broadening. "And sweat."

"That's because I've been waiting for you for over two hours," he chuckles. "I came here straight from the airport, but, as it's late, I didn't want to disturb your folks."

"So, yesterday when we spoke…"

"I was already in Atlanta, waiting for my connecting flight," he answers, his smile waning. "I started planning this trip that night we…that night you…"

She nods, not wanting him to further describe the awful evening their relationship had taken a southern turn.

"To say it hurt that you could think so little of me would be an understatement. It hurt me to my core." He tips up her chin. "But I understood your frustration. So, I finally engaged the expensive immigration lawyer I told you about, and, through her contacts, she helped get my P.R. issued. Apparently, I only needed to clarify some tax-related questions, and that was it."

"Praise God. Praise God!" Bianca says, still holding his face, a lump forming in her throat.

"I'm here for two months, and I'm not going back without us getting married and starting your paperwork," Prince says, his eyes holding hers. "We've waited long enough."

As his lips lower to hers, as they kiss for the first time despite being a couple for two years, and engaged for over one, all she can think is that the kiss…and him being there…have been worth waiting for.

April & Boma

"Well, thank God that's over," Boma says as he and April walk into his apartment that night. "Now, we can safely say we're more than halfway to us officially being married." He chuckles. "I guess that would make you a midwife."

THE MARRIAGE CLASS

April doesn't bother with the forced laughter she has resorted to in the weeks it has been since their marriage class began. It has been too much work, pretending to understand his jokes, forcing herself to laugh at them …and wishing he didn't expect her to.

His laughter fades as he takes a seat and reaches for the remote control, relieved not to hear her bogus laughter, but still disappointed he will never be able to laugh over quirky jokes with the woman set to be his wife. As she sits next to him, he reaches for her, eager for sexual release to quash his disenchantment. Because that seems to be the only language with which they can effectively communicate.

"No, Boma, please," she squirms out of his touch. "I haven't replaced my IUD. My doctor's appointment isn't till Tuesday."

"We're getting married in a matter of weeks," he says, burrowing his face in the hollow of her neck as his hands slide under her blouse. "Will it be the worst thing to get pregnant now?"

Her eyes widen in her horror and she pushes him off her. "Get pregnant how? I have no plans to get pregnant until I've completed my fashion styling course."

"What fashion styling course? You haven't even started it yet!" he retorts. Apart from a casual mention of her desire to take a course in Fashion Styling and Communication at the Accademia del Lusso in Milan, apart from the fact it is a three-year course, there has been no discussion about how that grand plan is to be funded.

"I intend to start right after the wedding, Boma. It's a hybrid of online and campus classes, so I should be able to swing it."

"Let me get this straight," he sits up, his eyes holding hers. "Assuming we had the money to pay for this - which we don't, by the way - you want us to wait three whole years before we start trying for kids?"

She shrugs. "We're still young."

"No, we're not, April," he says, deploying every atom of self-control he can not to raise his voice. "And even if we were, you don't think it's worth a conversation? This decision to wait not one, not two, but three years to have kids?"

"It's my body, and I don't need to have that discussion with anybody."

"Not even your husband?"

She sits up, eager to address the other thing he has said. "And what's this about us not having the money to pay for my course? Boma, I know how much you have in that domiciliary account of yours. So, you can't remove twenty thousand euros for your wife?"

"First of all, the fees are twenty thousand euros *per year!*" By now, he is exasperated enough for his voice to rise.

"Secondly, that money is for my business. How many times do I have to tell you that?"

"So, your wife is less important than your business?" she yells back. "Is that what you're saying?"

"Goddamit!" he exclaims, shooting to his feet, his hands on his head. "Is that honestly how you're processing this? Can't you see that if my business does better, I'll be able to give you so much more than twenty thousand euros?"

"What I'm 'processing' is how selfish you are," she answers, glaring at him. "I overlooked it when you insisted on cutting so many things from the wedding budget, but your refusal to pay for my course has shown me that you really only think about yourself!"

He stares at her with his mouth open, completely floored. Shaking his head, he runs his hands through his afro, and turns to her again. "April, what are we doing? We don't even like each other. Why do we want to put ourselves through a lifetime of hell?"

As she looks back at him, as much as she wants to yell, scream, demand that he take back his awful words, deep down, she knows he is saying the truth. They will make each other miserable.

"We're too different," he says, shaking his head again. "We're too different to make this work."

She looks away. As much as she hates to admit it...

He is right.

Ewa & Sanya

It is a little after 11am on Sunday morning when Sanya turns off Igede-Awo Road to the tarred road leading to Ewa's parents' house, after she surprised him with a text the previous night.

I've left for Osogbo. Come join me there tomorrow. There's something I'd like to show you.

The text message dropped a few minutes before midnight and he'd been tempted to ignore it, convinced it was another harebrained scheme of hers to extract more money from him. After a luxury goods trader who claimed Ewa owed her millions of naira for items she had purchased dragged her on social media, Sanya had sat his fiancée down, gotten her to itemize all the monies she owed. Seeing the eight-figure amount had stunned him speechless but, accepting that her debt would soon be as good as his, he'd cleared all of it, paying off every one of her irate creditors while at the same time demanding she make changes, the first being that she was to desist from purchasing anything on credit. Whatever she couldn't immediately pay for from what she earned as an influencer or from the allowance he gave her, she didn't need. The second was prohibiting her from using her 'glam squad' for non-sponsored social media posts. If a brand wasn't paying for the post, she would have to make do with her own makeup and styling skills. As a compromise, he'd agreed to take up Alaba's salary, seeing that both Ewa and her young protégée had grown very fond of each other.

So, reading her message, he could only imagine what kind of trouble she'd gotten herself into that had made her run all the way back home to Osogbo.

Osogbo.

Approaching the blue and white building with fuchsia pink bougainvillea flowers framing and spilling from its fence, he smiles, thinking about his earlier request to get married there. Even though, with each passing day, his desire for a quiet wedding with only their close friends and family in attendance, far away from brown-nosing socialites wanting to see and be seen, has grown, he has long accepted the implausibility of such a yearning, not with their wedding now less than three months away, and especially not with the kind of woman he is set to marry. If he knows Ewa well, she has every plan to break the Internet come September 10th, and that she cannot do from Osogbo.

"*E kaaro*, Sir," Sanya says, prostrating in greeting as the house keeper lets him into the living room, where Professor Fadairo, aka Prof, Ewa's father, sits in his wheelchair.

"Ah, good morning, my son," the man's bright smile is wide. "It's always a pleasure to see you."

"How is mommy? She's out?" Sanya asks.

"Ewa and her mother left the house as early as 8am this morning," Prof answers, gesturing at a chair. "Please, sit. Let us get you some breakfast. Some akara and ogi?" Without waiting for an answer, he turns to the housekeeper, who is still loitering at the door. "Iyabo, *mu oúnjẹ wá fún un.*"

Not one to decline a good meal, especially not fresh akara, Sanya nods in acceptance, his smile broadening a few minutes later as the tray with a plate of piping hot akara and a steaming bowl of white ogi adorned with yellow streaks of milk and a heaped tablespoon of sugar, is placed in front of him. Taking a spoonful of the sweet, soothing, fermented corn pudding, it is worth the four-hour drive.

"Get him more," a delighted Prof instructs Iyabo when he sees Sanya polish both the akara plate and ogi bowl.

"*E ṣe*, Ma," Sanya says to the elderly housekeeper, handing her the tray, happy to enjoy another serving of the delicious meal.

"Please, eat as much as you want, if it will take the edge off this wedding planning hassle. The thing is stressing everyone out," Prof remarks. "Especially now that it's happening here."

"Happening here?"

"Much better for me than going all the way to Lagos, but still incredibly stressful," Prof continues. "Look how early my wife had to leave the house. And she's been doing that all week, not just today."

THE MARRIAGE CLASS

The sound of a car driving into the compound punctuates the older man's rambling, and the door soon opens to admit Ewa's mother, an older, shorter, and curvier version of her daughter, with bright eyes and smooth skin that bely her almost sixty years of age. Sanya hits the floor in prostration and is pushing himself to his feet, when his eyes land on Ewa. He is transfixed to the spot, hunched with his fingers still touching the floor, but his eyes on her. With her hair slicked back into a scanty ponytail and wearing a silk tie and dye kaftan, Ewa is barefaced and glowing, the illumination from the sun from the open door enveloping her like a halo.

She smiles and rushes to him. "You came!"

He stands straight and holds her in a brief embrace, not wanting to prolong it out of respect for her parents, but also so that he can get a better glimpse of her face. Her hair is thin in its ponytail, her hairline about an inch or two receded, and her face shiny from the combination of its natural oils and sweat.

But she has never looked more beautiful to him than she does at that very moment.

"Ah, *oko mi*," Ewa's mother beams at him. "Looking ever handsome. Deji, if he weren't marrying our daughter, you would have competition oh."

Ewa smiles at Sanya, their gaze not breaking even with her mother's teasing, no longer feeling as ill at ease and sick to her stomach standing before Sanya in her truest and most authentic form, his captivation evident from his fixed gaze and parted mouth, the first time he is seeing not only her face without makeup, but her damaged and broken hair, the feature she is most self-conscious about.

"You like?" she asks.

His eyes drop to her lips, softer and more inviting without the sheen they always wear, and he smiles back. Oh, yes, he likes. He likes very much.

"Come," she says, taking his hand. Then turning to her parents. "We'll be back."

He allows her lead him to the back of the house and the sight there takes his breath away. The overgrown grass has been cut, giving an even better view of the neighboring cassava plantation and Ado Hill; both views rustic, both views picturesque.

"We'll erect a small marquee on the other side of the compound on the 8th, for the traditional wedding. But there will be a larger one out here on the 10th, for the white wedding," Ewa says. "Ndidi has sent some suggestions for how we can get the best of this view even with a marquee."

Ndidi is her decorator.

"What's going on, Ewa?"

She looks at him and her heart melts anew for this man. After she'd been forced to come clean to him about the extent of her financial mess - *all* of it - she'd been blown away when he'd underwritten her debt, paying off all fourteen million, three hundred and fifty thousand naira of it. Even as he had reeled off the things she needed to do to ensure that kind of thing never repeated itself, the only thing on her mind had been what she could do for him, how she could express her deepest gratitude to him. And if getting married in Osogbo would do that, then she was more than happy to.

"You were right about Logan Hall's full refund policy," she answers, smiling. "And my mom has found an exceptional caterer in Ife. All the other vendors - Ndidi, the photographers, the DJ, the MC, all of them - are ready to come to Osogbo."

A slow smile forms on his face. "You'd do that? You'd give up your Bella Naija wedding to get married here?"

She takes his hand and raises it to her face, her eyes still on him. "Celebrating our love is the most important thing. Even if it's under a rock, all I want is to be your wife."

Not caring that there is a perfect view of the backyard from her parents' living room, he pulls her into a kiss, feeling the most connected with her than he ever has.

ADESUWA O'MAN NWOKEDI

Kris & Bola

Four Weeks Before

"I don't think you have the kind of thick skin you need to be with an older woman."

Kris's words hang in the air for the rest of the ride to her Ikoyi home, overpowering even the music playing from the radio. In her compound, once Bola's car draws up in front of her house, she gets out and walks up to her front door without even a backward glance to see if he is following. He knows all he needs to do is start his car, drive away, and forget the whole thing. Maybe it will be easier to just do that; walk away. It will certainly be easier than having to constantly explain to everyone why he has chosen to marry a woman a decade and a half older.

He'd left out the detail of her age when he took Kris to meet his mother and siblings the first time. As beautiful as Kris had looked in an embroidered kaftan and long braids wrapped atop her head chignon style, as charmed as his family had been by her, with her jokes and funny anecdotes, not to mention the delicious carrot cake she had brought along, that she was an older woman was something that could not be hidden.

"She's how old?" his mother exclaimed, when he'd told her later that night after she'd prodded. "Forty what? Adebola!"

THE MARRIAGE CLASS

With his mother having just turned fifty-two, her horror was understandable. It had taken, surprisingly, his mother's twin sister, Aunty Taiwo, to convince her to give the woman her son had fallen in love with, a chance.

"She has a good aura, Kenny," Aunty Taiwo had said in placation to her twin. "Couldn't you feel it? I sure could. Isn't that's what's more important? For Adebola to marry a woman with a beautiful heart?"

"But a woman in her forties?" Bola's mother had protested, wide eyes dashing from her sister to her son, and back to her sister again. "What about children?"

"Women even older than her are having kids now," Aunty Taiwo countered. "Besides, many younger women struggle with fertility issues, so age is really no advantage these days." Turning to her nephew, a wide smile broke on her face. "He loves her, Kenny. Can't you see?"

Reluctantly, his mother had acquiesced, and in the months that followed, as Kris continued to work her charm with his family, his mother's acceptance was less reluctant and more wholehearted as a friendship bloomed between the two women.

With Kris's family, it had been a different kind of awkwardness when he and his family went to meet them in their Asaba home. From their furrowed brows and cocked heads, everyone – her parents, uncles, and siblings, two older and one younger – was visibly puzzled, suspicious of his motives.

Now, months later, they are still suspicious, just as his siblings and friends, despite their love for Kris, still question his choice of a woman who, under different circumstances, he could have called mother.

It will be easier to walk away than having her, this woman he has chosen, keep throwing missiles and expressing her never-ending doubt about their suitability for each other. If she really feels she's too old for him, is there any need to keep holding on and trying to convince her she's wrong? Is there any use trying to convince her he is *not* too young for her, and she is *not* too old for him? Won't it be easier to just walk away?

But as he watches her twist the keys three times in the lock to open her door, he knows it will not. He knows walking away from her will break him. He knows he loves her too much not to fight for this love with every breath he has.

"I don't need a thick skin to be with you," he calls out as he gets out of the car, loud enough for her to hear, and for her security guard to crane his head in their direction.

She pauses before turning to him, and even though her face is set, aloof almost, there is expectation in her eyes.

"Neither of us needs a thick skin, Kris," he says, walking up to her. "Our love is all we'll need to face anything the world throws at us. And God knows I have more than enough of that love for both of us."

She swallows hard, trying to fight off the tears that are threatening. She has not cried over a man in ten years, and she doesn't intend to start tonight. "You might change your mind when…"

"When never, Kris!" he exclaims, reaching for her hands. "Babe, you're stuck with me. I'm going to love you forever, so you better get used to that."

She smiles just as a tear, and then another, then several, roll down her face. "Forever?"

He grins as he tips up her face. "Forever to infinity, Kristina Ofili."

As she bursts into tears, he wraps her in an embrace, burying his face in her twisted-out curls, wanting to protect and love her eternally. "And I'm going to need more space in the closet if I have to move here."

"Done!" she giggles. "I'll clear out a quarter of the walk-in for you."

"Half, or no deal."

"As if you have enough clothes for half!" she laughs, smacking him on the chest. "You better take what I'm offering before I withdraw it."

"You drive a hard bargain soon-to-be Mrs. Bashua. But I'll take it!"

As they walk into the house, his arm over her shoulders and hers around his waist, they are united in their desire for each other…and to never again do anything to compromise their love.

Chioma & A.K.

Three Weeks Before

"Every single person we have ever come across wonders what on earth you see in me."

"Why the fuck should I be bothered what people *wonder* what I see in you when I *know* what I do?"

"It's getting too much for me, A.K. It's getting too much. I'm tired of constantly trying to do everything to look and sound good when we're together, trying, to no avail I might add, to make the staring from strangers stop. And I'm tired. I'm tired, A.K."

"So, what are you saying, Chioma? What exactly are you saying?"

They stand there in the kitchen; him staring at her, his heart racing as her words sink in, and her with eyes cast down, unable to look at him as she does the thing her heart is pleading with her not to, but which her head is screaming at her to - walk away. But for her resolve to stay strong, she knows she cannot look at him.

Or she will unravel.

"I don't know how else you want me to show you that I love you," he says, physically, mentally, and emotionally exhausted. "I really don't know what more you want me to say or do."

The weariness in his voice makes her look up.

"But one thing I do know is that I'm not going to be with someone who throws threats around like candy from a vending machine. I'm not going to live my life holding my breath anytime someone looks at you a certain way, or says something you don't like. Heck, if you're issuing threats now, what happens when the real serious things happen? What happens when we're faced with *actual* marriage difficulties? What happens then?" He sighs and empties the rest of his soda in the sink before tossing the empty can in the bin. "I have nothing more to say to you."

He walks out of the kitchen, leaving her stunned. In all the time they have been together, for every time she has voiced her insecurities, he has never failed to reassure her, never failed to express his love for her, never failed to remind her she is the one he chose, the only one he has ever been drawn to enough to make the commitment of forever. He has never walked away, leaving her with her insecurities. He has never called her bluff before.

Like he has now.

In a daze, she goes to the living room, slips into her shoes, and grabs her handbag. She'd had no intention of going home that night, planning to spend the rest of the week there. But, at 10:25pm, she finds herself summoning a taxi on the app on her phone, letting herself out of the house when it arrives, and sitting in the twenty-five minute ride to her Elegushi apartment. It is past 11pm when she lets herself into her flat, and as she stands in the darkness, the realization that she has finally pushed A.K. away makes her crumble to the floor in a heap. No matter how strongly she'd felt about her unsuitability for him, if she is to be true to herself, what she'd really hoped for was *even more* reassurance, *even more* declaration of his love. But it has turned out to be one too many toss of a coin into the river, and this time, A.K. has chosen not to dive in to fetch it. He has chosen to allow it sink instead, and that is enough to send her hyperventilating. She clutches her chest as she struggles to breathe, the heavy ring on her left finger the reminder of what she has thrown away. Curling into a fetal position on the floor fully dressed, she cries herself hoarse.

A.K. lies awake in bed all night, unable to shut his eyes. He hadn't expected her to leave and hearing the slam of the front door had made him peer out of the window of his study where he'd retreated to after their row. Seeing her actually get into a taxi at 10:30pm had incensed him, his rage over her lackadaisical approach to their relationship mounting, furious over how easily and frequently her suggestions that a breakup is in their better interest have come, hating how quick she is to repeat this, even after promising not to.

But most of all, hating how lowly she thinks of herself, hating how quick she is to call herself disparaging names, hating how she doesn't believe she is worthy of him. When, in fact, he is the one who isn't worthy of her.

While most of his life has been lived selfish and promiscuous, hers has been anything but. From that first night they talked until dawn at the beach, being with her has made him feel content, safe, and happy…so very happy. To him, her beauty is total and complete, inside and outside. While she thinks of her eyes as large and unattractive, he finds them mesmerizing, hypnotic almost. While she tries to do everything to mask the size of her lips, he loves the way they move when she talks and how they curve when she smiles, a magical smile that makes him want to do everything to keep it there. She is beautiful to him, and not just in abstract. Whether first thing in the morning, or when she is all dressed up, all he wants to do is look at her…hold her…be with her.

But he is tired of it, tired of constantly having to prove his feelings and loyalty to her. Yes, it hurts now, but maybe it is better to part while they are still ahead.

But as he tosses and turns in his bed all night, he knows he can neither walk away from the relationship nor stop loving her. By 5am, he rises to his feet, walks to the bathroom, splashes cold water on his face, swishes around some mouthwash, changes into a fresh t-shirt and pair of track downs, and makes his way downstairs, out the house, and into his car.

Because he would much rather spend forever reassuring her than not having her in his life at all.

The sound of knocking on her door awakens her, but she doesn't stir from her lying position on the floor. The knocking sounds like it is coming from a far distance, maybe even her dream, a vivid dream where she has been sprinting through some kind of maze, looking for A.K., yelling his name but failing to find him, running instead into walled dead ends over and over again.

"Chioma, please open the door."

The definite sound of his voice makes her eyes open and she sits up, still uncertain if it is some kind of dream, hallucination, or trance. But there is only one way to find out. Scrambling to her feet, she rushes to the door and opens it. Standing in the hallway is a disheveled A.K. But disheveled though he is, with bagged eyes and uncombed hair, he has at least changed his clothes, which is more than she can say for herself. She is now all too aware of how scruffy she looks, with her tousled hair, wrinkled clothes and – dear Lord - she is still wearing her loafers from the previous day.

He sees her give herself a once over and reaches for her before her over-analysis sets in. She needs no further prompting as she dissolves into his arms.

"I'm in love with you, Chioma," he says as they embrace. "And nothing is ever going to change that. You have to believe me." His voice breaks. "You're my whole world and losing you would kill me."

She shuts her eyes as she holds him, his words a soothing balm.

And, for the very first time, she believes him.

THE MARRIAGE CLASS

Nkoyo & Nosa

I'm sorry for not replying any of your messages or taken your calls. I just needed time to accept that you're really getting married to someone else. But I've reached that acceptance now, and I'm really happy for you, Noddy. You're going to be a great father and an amazing husband. I hope your fiancée knows how lucky she is.

Nosa reads the text message from Demi for probably the hundredth time since it dropped in his phone earlier that evening, hearing her voice as if she is there, speaking the words.

And his heart aches.

"I'm so glad marriage class is over," Nkoyo is saying, her legs stretched over his as they sit in the living room of the home they will soon share. "I'm not going to miss going to the mainland twice a week, that's for sure."

He nods, barely listening, his eyes still on the screen of his phone, reading the message yet another time, dissecting every word, searching for every nuance, every meaning the message does - and does not - contain.

"I was thinking it would be a good idea for us to travel somewhere," Nkoyo says, sliding closer and nestling her head on his shoulder, curving her hands around his arm.

"Just you and I. A babymoon, as they call it." She laughs, amused by the word she heard that afternoon for the first time, when she was checking destination options with her travel agent. "There are great deals for weekend trips to Ghana, The Gambia, and even Nairobi. It'll be fun."

It will be a chance for them to focus on each other and forget about wedding planning and baby preparations, a chance for him to ravage her body like he once did, a chance for her to remind him why he once found her so irresistible he couldn't keep his hands off her, not even when they were at work. Because he hasn't as much as kissed her since the day she broke the news of her pregnancy. Not even the times she has deliberately stripped herself stark naked before him, not even the times she has crawled into bed with him, asking…begging…him to make love to her.

"That can't be good for the baby," has been his constant excuse, and not even the explanation that not only will sex not harm the baby in any way, her raging hormones have made her desperate to feel him inside her again, taking her as wild and rough as he used to before. It is the reason she has set aside money she scarcely has to treat him to the weekend getaway she hopes will fix all that.

"That's nice," he says, gently detaching himself from her hold as he stands, walking across the room to the water dispenser, his eyes still on his phone.

"Maybe we can plan it for next weekend," Nkoyo prods, eager to see some kind of reaction from him; excitement, eagerness, heck even skepticism. Anything but this indifference.

But, again, she is disappointed.

"Sure," he answers perfunctorily, reading Demi's message yet again. That Demi addressed him with the nickname she'd coined for him back then, Noddy, makes him both happy and sad. It was a nickname she gave him their first year of dating, when he kept nodding off to sleep anytime they went to church together, and even though he is glad that she has used the endearment, it saddens him that he will never hear her call him that name again.

Nkoyo watches him as his eyes continue to scan the screen of his phone, and her heart sinks in painful realization.

"She got in touch with you, didn't she?" she asks. "Your ex."

He looks up and his rapid blinking is all the confirmation she needs.

"That look on your face," Nkoyo continues. "I remember it from the day I walked into your office and you were on the phone with her. I remember it from the times I'd see you talking to her before we…before we hooked up. You always had that look on your face." She shakes her head and smiles. "That look was there those amazing weeks we were hooking up. I remember waking up and seeing that look on your face as you watched me. You couldn't take your eyes or hands off me then."

Nosa clears his throat, puts the phone on the dining table, and shoves his hands into his pockets.

"Are you ever going to look at me like that again, Nosa?" Nkoyo asks, her eyes holding his. "I know you agreed to this marriage out of compulsion to do the right thing, but are you ever going to see me as more than just a wife on paper, but your partner and *lover*. You might not love me now, but is there a chance, any chance at all, of you ever loving me like you still love her?"

He shuts his eyes and sighs. It is a question he has asked himself many times, a fear he has nursed from the very moment he caved and agreed to marry her. But opening his eyes, he knows he can't lie to her anymore.

And he shakes his head.

Ivie & Eric

Two Weeks Before

"Don't talk as if you don't know how I feel about this whole thing. Need I remind you that you're the one who gave me a 'marry me or else' ultimatum. You know very well this is one rodeo I don't care to ride a third time."

As their eyes hold, Ivie's and Eric's, she accepts she is fighting a losing battle. As much as she wants him, and she does, as much as she wants to be with him forever, and she does, she doesn't want it like this. So, she slips off the platinum diamond ring from her finger and drops it on the coffee table.

Eric clenches his jaw as she sets the ring, the ring he spent a tidy fortune on, on the coffee table. "If you do that, we're done, Ivie. I'm not here for these childish, petty games. If you leave that here, it'll be the last time you ever see it."

She smiles, even as her eyes pool with tears. "Of course, you won't play my 'childish, petty games' or, as it is for men in real, committed relationships, fight for me. It doesn't surprise me at all." She shrugs. "Well, I release you, Eric. I release you from this rodeo, circus, spectacle, inconvenience, and all the other words you've had for what, to me, has just been wanting to love you forever."

He grunts and reaches for the remote control, tapping the volume increase button, trying to return his attention to the game he is watching, hating that, beneath the anger, irritation, and impatience he feels over her display, lurks an emotion very alien to him.

Fear.

As he struggles to stay focused on the game, even as Vinícius Júnior nets a goal for Real Madrid in the fifty-ninth minute, he tries not to notice as Ivie picks up her handbag from the credenza, as she walks to the door and slips on her shoes. His nostrils flare as he hears the click of her heels in the hallway and as the front door opens, letting her out, wanting to feel relieved that the noose around his neck has been removed, and that he will not have to go through the, yes, inconvenience of yet another marriage. But all he feels is hollow, the realization their relationship is over making him feel like someone in a chokehold. Grunting, he switches off the television. No woman has ever been indispensable to him, and Ivie will not be the first. If his first two breakups didn't kill him, breakups that each cost him a fortune and several lost years with his children – Emily and Brian from his first wife, Imelda, didn't speak to him for three years after the divorce, and his relationship with Jason, his son from his second wife, Ashiedu, is still on the path to recovery six years after that marriage ended – this one, this breakup with Ivie, will most surely not.

Going up to his bedroom, he undresses, happy to have been spared the usual back and forth of Ivie pleading to sleep over, relieved not to have to explain, yet again, why he would rather sleep alone. Having spent half of his life married, eloping with Imelda when he was only twenty-three years old and marrying Ashiedu when the ink on his first divorce wasn't even dry, he has relished being able to fall asleep without the sound of another person breathing or, worse, snoring. He has loved being able to stretch out, spread-eagled if he wants, on his bed. He has delighted in leaving the reading light on for as long as he wants, without being nagged to turn it off. He has savored the sound of silence, allowing his own thoughts run wild and free.

But that night, the silence is deafening, the solitude consuming, and he lies awake, staring at the ceiling, his eyes unable to shut. Getting off the bed, he grabs a cigar and walks across the room, sliding open the door that leads to the veranda overlooking the Ikoyi Link Bridge. Lighting up the cigar, as he inhales, he knows forgetting Ivie will be harder than he thought.

He never should have allowed things get this far.

"Please, forget that old man!" Urenna, Ivie's best friend, says as they talk on the phone that night. She has never liked Eric. "It's long overdue, *abeg*! You've wasted enough time with that narcissist."

"But I love him," Ivie says, cradling her phone and sitting cross-legged on her bed well after midnight, the splintering of her heart an actual ache in her chest.

"Fuck love! What you need is a man without all that baggage!" Urenna answers. "Listen, tomorrow, you're coming with me for a party at Eko Atlantic, a bachelor's eve. You're going to come out, and you're going to start meeting new people. You'll find yourself a better man, way better than that arrogant bastard."

Ivie wipes a tear from her face, thinking she would do anything to be back with that arrogant bastard. She rubs a finger over the now bare one, the one that, until two hours before, had housed her beautiful diamond ring. And she is broken anew.

"I know it hurts, but you'll get over it, hun." Her older sister, Igho, is more sympathetic when they talk minutes after her conversation with Urenna is over.

"I love him, Igho," Ivie says, her voice breaking as tears roll down her face. "I love him."

"Oh, darling, I know you do," Igho coos. "I know you do, but if you're not happy now, getting married won't fix that."

Ivie nods, sobbing at the same time. As much as it is killing her now, being treated as a bothersome inconvenience for the rest of her life is not an option.

At 6am the next morning, as her eyes open, she contemplates skipping her daily morning run, the desire to lie in bed under her sheets not only for the rest of the morning but, indeed, the rest of the weekend, tempting. The reminder of the implosion of her relationship, her engagement, her love affair with the man of her dreams, squeezing her heart and pressing down on her chest, making it almost impossible to breathe. Realizing that painful reminder is what will be her companion that morning, and not the sleep she seeks as an escape, she pushes off her comforter and gets out of bed.

Fifteen minutes, she is jogging down Admiralty Way, turning right on to the Link Bridge. Her eyes travel to the Banana Island side of the lake that the bridge traverses, and she wonders what Eric is doing, if he is going about his normal routine of running on his treadmill while listening to the *We Study Billionaires* podcast, or if he is equally as shattered about what has happened between them. The last time they broke up, when she'd walked out on him at his friend's wedding, he'd shown up in her house less than an hour later. But this time, several hours later, there hasn't even been a text message from him, talk less of a phone call or a visit. So, it is safe to assume that pining for her is something he isn't doing that morning. Pummeling faster on her run, she bites her lower lip to keep any tears from making a reappearance that morning. It's a new dawn, a new day.

Time for new beginnings.

Listening to Stig Brodersen and Trey Lockerbie interview financial guru, Katie Gatti about building a wealth plan for financial independence, Eric can only manage a trot on the treadmill in his home gym. Reaching for his phone, he is disappointed not to have received the video Ivie would have sent by now, the one she sends after completing her run every morning, grinning and sweat-faced, telling him just how many calories her app says she has burned and challenging him to better it. Today, there is no video from her, no text message. Instead, all he sees on his screen are notifications from his secondary school's WhatsApp group, a group he keeps meaning to archive with its never-ending messages spamming his phone. Putting down the phone, he ramps up the speed of the treadmill and quickens his pace to a sprint.

The pain is temporary, but it will pass.

It has to pass.

And this is what he reminds himself as the weekend goes by, and as he walks into his office building on Monday. As he settles down to work, it feels strange not to have already spoken to her that morning, not to have heard her encourage him for his day ahead, not to have asked his secretary to buy her flowers. He struggles to stay focused in his meetings, struggles to pay attention to his Chief Financial Officer in the debrief about the month gone by and plans for the one just begun. And, that evening, as he sits alone at Atmosphere restaurant, eating their signature roast potatoes and steak meal, rather than be relieved about being finally released from the excruciating chore their marriage class in Yaba has been, he finds himself missing it.

Missing her.

Accompanying Urenna for the party is a great idea. It is Ivie's chance to dress up and leave the house. And as she socializes, the first time alone in three years, the attention she receives is enough to make her feel good about herself, enough to make her forget her heartache, even if only for a few hours. She takes so many pictures - with Urenna and with her new friends - and later that evening, without an outlet for them, proceeds to upload them to her personal Instagram account, an account that has been largely dormant since she assumed her role as Client Relationship Vice President for the global marketing company,

THE MARRIAGE CLASS

Aphrodite, three years ago, when her focus shifted, instead, to their clients' social media pages. Now, as she uploads the pictures and videos from the evening, she starts believing that light might truly be at the end of the tunnel. She reminds herself of that later that night, when the pain descends on her as she lies in bed, and the next night when she feels so broken, all she wants to do is pick up the phone and call Eric, and the following Monday when she walks into her apartment, painfully aware of the marriage class they are missing, the class on Conflict Management she had looked forward to.

Pouring herself a glass of wine and settling into her sofa to continue watching the *Blood Sisters* series on Netflix, she chants the mantra she has now adopted, the mantra that this, too, shall pass, the mantra that this pain, too, will go away.

The following Friday, swimming in the Ikoyi Club pool, his legs kicking and arms spinning through the water, Eric seeks the buoyancy and sense of freedom the water moving around his limbs in swirls, creates. Except this time, there is no freedom, and, even underwater, the visual of Ivie's face is just as clear as if she is swimming right by him, as if she has taken residence there in the cobalt blue water.

Getting out of the pool, he notices the appreciative glance of a woman lying reclined on a sunlounger, and he smiles. With his strict diet and exercise regimen, his lean, firm, and athletic body makes him look younger than his fifty-three years of age. She returns the smile and waves, giving him a clear opener to hone in on her. She doesn't look a day older than twenty-five and, if her large Dior sunglasses are anything to go by, is a lover of the finer things of life. With little effort on his part, she could be in his bed that night. So, why is he wasting time thinking about his ex-girlfriend when he can have any woman of his choice? Why is he thinking about the damned marriage class they are missing right now, and not chatting up this sexy young thing? Why can't he stop obsessing about Ivie, for crying out loud?

Giving the woman a small nod, he looks away and heads to his bench, picks up his towel and pats himself dry. Reaching for his phone, as he has been doing in the last few days since realizing Ivie has started posting on her Instagram page again, he heads straight there and, yep, new pictures have been added since the last time he checked. She and her annoying friend, Urenna, are dining at a restaurant, SLoW Lagos from the look of things, and she has captured everything from their food, to their drinks, to cheesy selfies of the pair of them. His brows furrow, recognizing the Lobster Tail Thermidor meal she has ordered for herself and wondering why she hasn't opted for the Beef Milanese that is her favourite on that menu, wondering why she is drinking a Pedro and Zobo cocktail instead of her usual herbal gin and tonic. But it is the pictures with her face he is unable to take his eyes off, pictures of her smiling wide, of her laughing hard, of her neck thrown back the way it typically does when she laughs. Scrolling through the other pictures on her page, pictures added in the past week, pictures he has already seen and obsessed over, pictures of her on her morning run, selfies by her car showing off her outfit of the day, snapshots of her at work with her colleagues, out with friends for lunch...dinner...drinks, she is living her best life. She is happy, and the realization that she isn't even mourning their relationship at all makes his heart bleed.

The banner atop his screen makes him do a double take. Ivie Eghe-Osagie is starting a live video? Since when has she started going live on Instagram? Without thinking twice, he taps on the banner to join. Ivie is still seated at SLoW and is talking and waving her hands in her usual animated manner. There are already thirty-six people watching the live video, a number which rapidly grows as the seconds tick.

"Seriously, guys, the food here is amazing! I've been here many times, but it is my first time really stepping out of my comfort zone and ordering new things," she is saying, beaming as she holds up her phone. "And I can't believe I never had the courage to try them earlier."

His chest constricts, wondering if she is talking about the food...or their relationship.

"Like this Pedro and Zobo cocktail," she lifts up her glass. "I mean, listen guys, listen! This drink is the gospel truth!" She turns the phone to her companion's drink. "Urenna is having the...what's it called again?"

"Ginger and Lychee martini," her friend answers.

The camera zooms to the cloudy, frothy drink, with a round slice of lime garnishing the rim of the glass.

"Babe, I'm going to have that next," comes Ivie's voice, before the camera cuts back to her face. "Guys, this is going to be my *third* drink!"

"It's Friday, and the night is still young!" Urenna's loud voice booms across.

Ivie laughs and shakes her head. "Stay tuned to see whether I do, or don't, call it a night." She taps a finger on her chin, as if in contemplation. "But anyway, guys, don't forget you can recreate these cocktails with Pop Cherry soda. Also, don't forget that a new Burger Chef opens tomorrow on Akin Adesola Street. Make sure you come. You won't regret it."

Eric can't help but smile, amused how she hasn't missed the chance to take advantage of the one hundred and seventeen people now watching her live video, to promote not one, but two of her company's clients.

With a wave, she winks. "Bye, guys!"

And the video ends.

Exasperated, Eric wants to throw the phone into the pool, frustrated not knowing if she truly intends to party all night, aggravated about the thought of her meeting another man while out, about the thought of her dating such a man…falling for him…marrying him.

THE MARRIAGE CLASS

The thought of her marrying someone else makes him literally stop breathing for a split second. It is an alien feeling to him, considering how he hasn't cared less when or whom his ex-wives have moved on with. He'd been completely unbothered when Imelda remarried ten years after their divorce, attending her wedding and even gifting her and her new husband a holiday to the Maldives. As for Ashiedu and her constant thirst traps on Instagram, pictures of her in skimpy bikinis, showcasing a body that has visited a few too many plastic surgeons, holidaying around the world, often with some muscled toy boy or the other, apart from feeling sorry for the embarrassment caused their sixteen-year-old son, all Eric has felt seeing her pictures has been indifferent…slightly amused maybe, but mostly indifferent.

But there is nothing indifferent about how he now feels, seeing Ivie's pictures.

And sitting there on the sunlounger, one week after the end of their relationship, he realizes he has made the biggest mistake of his life letting the only woman he has ever truly loved slip away.

As Urenna punches her passcode into the payment terminal the waiter holds, Ivie's eyes flit to the table by the window facing the garden, the table where she and Eric would have been seated if they had come together, and the all-too-familiar ache crushes her insides. She sees them how they would have been; him in his usual smart suit, usually black, and her in whatever she'd worn to work that day, him sipping his gin and tonic in between telling anecdotes of his day, and her laughing so hard her eyes would tear. Her eyes are tearing now, but it isn't from laughter.

"Moyo, Ebun, and Ebere are waiting for us at Vibe," Urenna says, glancing at her wristwatch. "We'll take more pictures there, and do another live video."

"He saw this one," Ivie says, her eyes widening as she sees *mr_orizu* as one of its viewers. She looks up at Urenna. "Eric saw this one."

Even though she knows he is active on Instagram, Twitter, and even TikTok, to keep up with what his children are up to, it never crossed her mind Eric would actually take any notice of her posts, let alone her live video.

"I told you he would. Useless man!" Urenna snorts. "And we have to do many more to pepper him. We need to show him you're living your best life and that he can piss off forever, for all we care."

Ivie's eyes drop to her screen, looking at his name again. The fact that he saw the video but still has not called lets her know she is doing anything but 'peppering' him. It has been a whole week without word from him, and his silence is speaking in volumes louder than any of his words ever did. It's also not helping that they are missing their second class, the penultimate one before the course ends next week. And any hopes she might have nursed about a turnaround in his stance, a softening of his heart, come crashing down with the realization that, by missing two classes, and likely a third, their chances of getting married are now even slimmer.

"You guys can head out without me," Ivie says, forcing a smile. "I'm a bit tired and want to just go home to rest."

"Tired, *faya*!" Urenna retorts, pulling her to her feet. "We're going out tonight, you're going to have fun, and you're going to take pictures while doing it."

In spite of her melancholy, Ivie laughs, knowing her friend won't take no for an answer. Hoisting her handbag on her shoulder, she allows Urenna lead her out, smiling as they stop at the bar to exchange greetings with two guys sitting there, Urenna's work colleagues. As all four of them file out, headed to Vibe bar, Ivie makes up her mind to do all she can to enjoy herself and not let thoughts of Eric colour her evening.

She has already lost three years to him, besides.

The following Friday, two weeks after their breakup, as soon as the banner of her going live flashes across his phone, Eric taps it. Even though he has been tuning in to all her live videos, all the nine she has done since that first one at SLoW, documenting everything from being out with friends, to attending the launch of her client's fast-food restaurant, today is different. Today, he is tuning in not just to ogle her, but to see her location, to note where she is hanging out that Friday…and with whom.

"Hi, guys!" Ivie waves at her camera. "So, Urenna, Moyo, and I are at RSVP today. I've been here a few times," with him, "but today, just like I've been doing all week, I'd like to try something I haven't. So, recommendations are welcome."

Tapping off his phone, Eric beckons at Ibukun, the Associate he has roped in for his plan, a plan that could very easily backfire, a plan for which he is willing to take that risk.

"RSVP," Eric says to his driver, as he and Ibukun board the car. A few streets away from his office, luckily, it won't take long to get there.

"How come you're all recommending sushi?" Ivie giggles into her camera, amazed by the six hundred and twenty-three number of accounts currently viewing. "I don't eat sushi *oh*!"

"I thought you said you're open to trying something new," Moyo teases, looking at her with a raised brow.

"I draw the line at raw food," Ivie laughs. "So, next!"

THE MARRIAGE CLASS

The Mercedes-Benz G-Class pulls up in front of the restaurant's gates and Eric exhales, nervous more over getting rejected than the out-of-character stunt he is about to pull, but ready to do what he needs to, to dive right off the deep end if he has to, to win Ivie back. Handing his phone to Ibukun, he nods and exhales again.

"Do it. Just like we discussed."

"Okay, so I've ordered the Prawn Tempura starter, Lobster Gnocchi and Sweet Potato Fries for my main, and a Coconut Sorbet for dessert," Ivie says to the now over eight hundred people watching. "Urenna and Moyo have chosen to go down sushi road, and are both having a Prawn and Crab Maki. For drinks, we're all trying the Moscow Pony cocktail." Her grin widens. "I'll come back online when our orders get here. Wish us luck!"

Ending the broadcast, her smile fades and she exhales. Urenna and Moyo are gushing over a man who has just walked in, but rather than join them, all Ivie can think of is the last marriage class happening that very moment.

"I hope you're not going to be a Debbie Downer tonight," Moyo says, wagging a finger at her. "Can't you see the blessing in all this? Can't you see how many people join your live broadcasts every day? You're a natural at this and should consider taking this food and restaurant blogging more seriously."

But her voice fades when Ivie sees a banner flash on her screen, informing her *mr_orizu* has started a live video. Eric going live? Someone must have stolen his phone. She taps the banner and joins the less than ten people already watching it.

"I'm not sure how this works," he says, adjusting his jacket, his eyes travelling to whomever is holding his phone. "Do I start talking now or when I'm inside?"

"Now, Sir. To give your viewers context," comes a familiar voice she can't immediately identify.

Eric nods, clears his throat, nods again, and straightens his lapel again, his nerves apparent. Ivie watches, stunned, never having seen him anything but self-assured and composed before.

"Right," he clears his throat again as he walks, the person holding his phone struggling keep in step. "I'm here to get my girl."

His girl? He already has another girl? And he feels enough for this girl to do...to do this? Her heart begins a slow descent to her stomach as she watches him walk into...wait, is that RSVP's courtyard?

THE MARRIAGE CLASS

"Sir, keep talking," Ibukun says as they walk through the compound in the direction of the door.

"I'm here for my girl, I already said that," Eric answers, but the frown on Ibukun's face is his prompt to say more, lest he ruin the whole thing. "Because I messed things up with her. Because I miss her. Because I love her."

They enter the packed restaurant and he looks around, unsure where she is seated. Ibukun looks at him, waiting for direction.

The hostess smiles at them. "Do you have reservations, Sir?"

Eric stares at her, the same hostess that has received him at that same restaurant several times before, now suddenly short of words. He turns to Ibukun, who is also looking at him, waiting. He returns his attention to the hostess, hoping she can point him in Ivie's direction with a name or a description.

And then he sees her.

Looking up from her phone, her heart skips several beats as her eyes clap with Eric's. Urenna and Moyo stop talking as they see him, too. As Eric makes his way in her direction, Ivie's heart is thumping so hard in her chest, she fears she will pass out any minute. She sees Ibukun, one of his employees, retro-pedaling in front of him, holding up a phone, Eric's phone. Glancing at her screen, she sees his broadcast is still on, and, with shocking clarity, realizes *she* is the girl Eric is there for. He has come for her. Moyo smiles, picks up Ivie's phone, and starts a live broadcast.

"What's all this?" Ivie asks, when Eric and Ibukun get to their table.

"I've missed you, kid," Eric answers, with that lopsided smile that turns her to mush. "My life's no fun without you."

Ivie swallows hard, looking at Ibukun's phone, and now hers in Moyo's hand, both focused on her, and is equal parts angry and dazed, feeling like she is having an out-of-body experience.

"You made your position crystal clear," she answers, careful with her words, not wanting to divulge too much to the God-knows-how-many-people watching both broadcasts.

"I was afraid of getting in too deep, afraid of failing again," he answers, dropping to one knee. "But, it turns out, I'm already in deep over my head. I'm in love with you, kid."

There are gasps from Urenna, Moyo, Ibukun, and the people seated at a nearby table. Ivie's hands fly to her mouth, not daring to believe what is playing out before her, convinced it is surely a dream.

THE MARRIAGE CLASS

Eric looks at her from his half-kneeling position, his heart melting for her anew. With his first marriage, upon finding out she was pregnant, he and his Trinidadian girlfriend, Imelda, had walked into the Islington and London City Register office and married, both of them settling on cheap rings from Argos. With Ashiedu, thirteen years later, while shopping at the Westfield Mall, she had led him to the South African diamond store, Brown's, and picked herself a ring. As they had already been together a year, he'd decided to take the gamble with another marriage. And months ago, when Ivie had given him the ultimatum to marry her, he'd gotten her to send him a picture of the ring she wanted, ordering the platinum scalloped pavé diamond ring after she did. Never would he have ever thought himself doing the one thing he scorned other men for doing - getting down on one knee for a woman. But looking up at Ivie, he would have it no other way.

"What are you doing, Eric?" Ivie asks, shaking her head in her amazement, tears in her eyes. "In front of all these people?"

He takes her hand. "*Especially* in front of all these people. You are the light of my world and I want to get on this rodeo, perform in this circus, create this spectacle called marriage with you. I need you like a heart needs a beat." He winks and chuckles. "How's that for an ad copy?"

She laughs, she cries, her hands back to covering her mouth, taking in the fact that this is no dream, no mirage, no hallucination.

He reaches into his pocket and brings out her ring. "Loving you isn't one of my options, Ivie." The smile on his face wanes. "It's the only one. And I'm sorry it has taken me this long to see it. Please, marry me."

She nods, and the entire restaurant breaks into rapturous applause, phones clicking and flashing everywhere. Eric slips the ring on her finger, they rise and fall into an embrace, all the angst, trauma and pain of the last two weeks now a distant memory.

"You do know we've missed three whole classes, right?" she giggles in his ear, as they embrace.

He pulls back and tips up her chin. "I already have that covered, kid."

And then he kisses her.

Ogechi & Zulu

One Week Before

"Or what? Or what will happen? Be careful, Ogechi. In your better interest, I will advise you not to call my bluff."

Ogechi's mouth parts as she stares at him, speechless for several seconds. "Your bluff? Look at this local fool oh! Is it because I decided to stoop to your level? Imagine this one talking about bluff!" Then hitting her side of the door.

THE MARRIAGE CLASS

"Osita, stop this car. Stop this car and let me out right now!"

"But, Ma..." Zulu's driver pleads, his imploring eyes meeting hers in the rear view mirror.

"*Nwoke, mepee ụzọ*! Open the door for her right now, let her get out of my car!" Zulu yells, now irate, incensed by her insults.

Osita screeches to a halt on the expressway and Ogechi storms out of the car, slamming the door for good measure. As the Escalade zooms off, she glares at the car until it disappears from sight, standing haplessly on the sidewalk. Bringing out her phone, she orders an Uber, doing everything not to make eye contact with any of the curious drivers and passengers of cars whizzing by, knowing just how peculiar she looks, standing on the expressway surrounded by half a dozen bags of clothes and shoes. Thankfully, the black Honda Accord taxi pulls up in front of her less than ten minutes later, and they continue the remaining ten-minute drive to her VGC estate house.

The first thing she does when she gets home is call Chinasa.

"What kind of bush, foolish man did you introduce me to?" she hollers, even before her friend has a chance to say hello. "Is that how you and Nduka rate me?" Nduka is Chinasa's husband. "For you to think this kind of stupid lowlife will be my type?"

"Zulu is talking to Nduka right now," Chinasa says, her voice weary. "He has been shouting and complaining for almost thirty minutes. What did you do to him, Oge?"

Ogechi's eyes almost bulge right out of their sockets and her body vibrates in her rage. "What did *I* do to him? Why aren't you asking what he did to *me*?"

Chinasa sighs. "Zulu is a good man, Oge. You need to try to…"

Not waiting to hear the rest of her statement, Ogechi disconnects the line. The nerve of Chinasa! The nerve of the idiotic Zulu! The nerve of everyone who thinks she has to settle for less because of her age! Tomorrow, she will start the process of informing her family that the wedding, this senseless sham of a wedding, is off. She will absolutely not be marrying a brute like that.

But opening her eyes the next morning, she cannot quite bring herself to call her parents and burst her mother's bubble of joy. She decides to give herself a week for the idea to settle and marinade, so that when she does inform her parents, she will be in a better mental state to handle their disappointment.

And heading to work on Monday morning, as her ring flashes under a ray of early morning sun as she waits at a traffic light, the thought of taking it off, of explaining to her friends and colleagues that this long awaited marriage won't be happening, fills her with dread. She knows it will have to be done, but it doesn't have to be done right now, right? It, too, can wait another week, right?

THE MARRIAGE CLASS

Right.

Lying in bed that night, sipping on a cup of chamomile tea and scrolling through her TikTok feed, she giggles over the funny posts, relieved to have shed the heavy weight of being with a man who can't even make a complete sentence in English, a man who dresses like an utter clown and who would embarrass her for the rest of her life...or his, as she would kill him first for sure. She is much better off without him.

So much better off.

The next evening, lying in bed, she creates profiles on the dating sites Tinder, Bumble, and Hinge, ready to finally give online dating a try. She uploads several of her best pictures, pictures that showcase her generous figure and exquisite taste in clothes. She spends the rest of the evening swiping left, not impressed with any of the profiles she sees, the good looking men sounding like perverts, and the unattractive men...also sounding like perverts. It isn't until midnight that she happens on the profile of a good-looking, bespectacled, dark-skinned man - a doctor, if his title is anything to go by. From his interests – travelling, cooking, reading, and philanthropy – he doesn't sound depraved, and he is less than ten miles from her, making it even better. So, she swipes right.

Hey, gorgeous lady. His message drops less than ten minutes later.

Hi, she types, smiling. She decides to be brazen and adds ***I like your profile.***

I like yours too, he replies. *Your boobs are special. Are they real?*

She frowns at her screen, re-reading the message to be sure she has seen it right.

And that ass! Big, bold, and beautiful! You're a walking sex billboard, has anyone told you that?

Without further ado, she taps on the ellipses icon at the top right corner of her screen and hits the *Unmatch* button. She continues to scroll until she gets to the page of a smiling guy leaning on a car. His interests are crypto currency and landscaping and, at the risk of his idea of landscaping being shaving a woman's nether regions, she swipes right.

Hi, there.

A nice, simple opener. That has to be a good sign.

Hello, is all she types back. She has learned her lesson.

You're pretty. I can't believe my luck that I've matched with someone as hot as you.

Her smile broadens. *You don't look bad yourself.*

So, what do you do for a living?

She frowns, wondering if it isn't too direct for his very first question, but she chides herself for being paranoid.

I work in an investment bank here in Lagos, she answers. *You?*

THE MARRIAGE CLASS

A bit of this and that. Mainly crypto trading, as you can see from my profile.

Interesting.

Investment banker, huh? That must mean you're very rich. Hahahaha

Her upper lip curls on its own accord. *I do okay*, she manages to respond.

How much do you make a month? A million? Two? More?

Alarm bells start to sound in her head. *It's a little too early to be talking money, don't you think? We don't even know each other's last names.*

There is a long pause until, suddenly, the entire chat goes grey. And she realizes he has unmatched them.

Setting her phone down, her eyes still wide open even though it is now past 1am, she is reminded of one harsh reality. It's a jungle out there in the dating world.

The next evening, Wednesday, as her phone buzzes with messages from all three apps, the thought of checking any of them makes her sick to her stomach, the prospect of conversations like the night before almost giving her a panic attack. She decides Netflix will be a better companion that night, and as she watches a Kevin Hart comedy special, she struggles to focus, the jokes that would have had her in stitches barely eliciting a smile from her. Her phone's WhatsApp message notification chimes and she dives for it. It is only as she reads a reminder from

Chinasa for Nduka's forty-fifth birthday party on Saturday that she realizes whom she'd hoped the message was from. Scrolling to the last message Zulu sent her the morning of their photo shoot, she smiles as she reads it.

Obi'm, let's spend some together after this your photo shoot.

She smiles as she remembers how angry she'd been about his referencing the photo shoot as *hers*, but now, with fresh eyes, seeing that all he'd wanted was to spend time with her. She continues to scroll through his messages, all of them beginning with an endearment – *Achal'ugo, Obi'm, Nkem, Eggovin* – all of them expressing eagerness to see her, be with her…and she finds herself missing them.

She finds herself missing him.

The next morning, she calls Chinasa on the phone. "Will Zulu be at Nduka's party tomorrow?"

"Why won't he be here?" Chinsasa retorts. "You think because you're stupid enough to throw away a good man, we will do the same? He'll be here, so if it's a problem for you, you better stay in your house."

Well, she has no intention to stay in her house.

Stepping into Nduka and Chinasa's Dolphin Estate compound, Zulu's eyes scan the packed lawn for Ogechi, wanting to see her…dreading to see her. Even though her

THE MARRIAGE CLASS

words and actions the previous weekend ripped apart his already fragile confidence, he has spent the last week missing the sound of her voice, missing the smell of her skin that reminds him of something fresh out of a bakery, missing those eyes that turn his brain to butter. But he has never had to beg a woman for her company and he isn't about to start now. No matter how deeply he still feels for her, if she thinks she's too good for him, then she is free to move on to whomever will live up to her high standards. There are many fish in the sea, and Nduka has already intimated him of a lady his brother, Ikedi, plans to introduce him to tonight.

So, squaring his shoulders, his gift of a forty-year-old bottle of Glenfiddich whisky in hand, he marches past the merrymakers, in search of his friend.

Ogechi smells Zulu's strong oud perfume before she even sees him. Looking up from her sitting position in the living room, she sees him walk through the front door, watching as his face lights up upon sighting the birthday boy, Nduka, who in turn pulls him into an embrace, a noisy one with both men hailing each other in Igbo, praising each other with lofty traditional titles she is sure neither is qualified to have. They are so loud, some of the people seated in the living room throw irritated glances their way. Time was when Ogechi, too, would have been vexed by such a rowdy display, when the sight of Zulu wearing a fitted velvet top in a shade of purple no person of the male gender should be caught dead in, over a tight pair of black jeans, with ankle-high boots that have no utility in the tropics, would have made her sick with disgust. But not so tonight, not so. Tonight, as she looks at him, as she watches him laugh with his friend, as her heart warms from the familiarity of his face, his deep belly laughter, his habit of placing both hands on the shoulders of whomever he's talking to, she misses it…all of it. His grin, which she'd thought way too broad before, reveals a gap-toothed smile, and his thick eyebrows give his face character she has never noticed before, the mystique of not quite knowing if he is angry or amused. He is handsome from the depth of his eyes, to the genuineness of his smile, to the way his voice quickens as he talks. And as he hands Nduka his gift, she realizes his is a beauty that starts from his kind, loving, and generous heart, radiating from there everywhere else.

As if sensing her gaze, he looks in her direction. And as their eyes hold, his smile disappears and his eyes narrow.

His heart lurches in his chest upon seeing her, and he hates his body for its immediate betrayal, every nerve in it responding to the sight of her like a plant in a dry desert, desperate for a drop of water. Quickly, he looks away, returning his attention to Nduka, and Ikedi who has now joined them. Thankfully, they lead him away, to the patio where the other guys are seated.

The further away he can get from her, the better.

THE MARRIAGE CLASS

She watches with dismay as Nduka and his brother lead Zulu away, tempted to follow them, but aware how desperate that will make her look. He's the one who should be seeking her out. As a matter of fact, how dare he ignore her like he just did! No, she's going to sit right here and wait for him to come to her, on his knees, begging her to take him back.

"This is Anwuli," Ikedi says, standing before him with a tall, slim, light-skinned girl. "Anwuli, meet my friend, Zulu."

With a pointed chin and angular cheekbones softened by doe shaped eyes, a small button nose, pert lips with a pronounced Cupid's bow, and long, jet black hair that is all hers, Anwuli is breathtakingly beautiful. And from the way Ikedi is winking at him, not only does he know this, he is proud to be the one presenting Zulu with a gift like this.

"Hello, Anwuli," Zulu says to the girl, smiling even though all he wants to do is demand what a girl her age is looking for in a party for grown folks. She doesn't look a day older than twenty.

"Let me go join the others," Ikedi says, the other guys having relocated to the den to watch an old football game. "And give you two the chance to get to know each other," he adds with another exaggerated wink. As he walks away, he mouths at Zulu *no slack oh!*

Anwuli has her back to Ikedi so doesn't see his foolishness. Zulu purses his lips, hoping that is enough to communicate to his friend's brother his disinterest in participating in pedophilia with a girl half his age. But as she takes a seat next to him, he knows deep down that her age is just an excuse. Seeing Ogechi again has thrown him, leaving him with little or no interest in meeting anyone else that night.

"I've heard a lot about you," Anwuli says, smiling at him, her voice sonorous. "Ikedi and Nduka have nothing but nice things to say about you."

Zulu nods, his smile only polite. "All lies, I'm sure." He observes her keenly. "Are you a student?"

"Do I look that young?" she giggles, her hand dropping to his knee. "I'm a lawyer. I just got called to the bar."

Her answer does little to change his opinion, his eyes going where her hand now rests on his knee. Since when have women been this forward?

"How old are you?" It is more of an accusation than a question.

"I'll be twenty-three next Thursday," she leans forward to whisper in his ear, her fruity floral fragrance enveloping him. "Should I expect a birthday present from you?"

THE MARRIAGE CLASS

Unable to contain herself, Ogechi stands up and walks in the direction of the dining room in search of Zulu. Almost an hour has gone by and there is no indication of him coming to look for her. As much as she would like to retain the upper hand, she cannot afford for either of them to leave that night without speaking…and making amends. Because if the last few days have shown her anything, it is that she doesn't want to lose him.

And that she is in love with him.

He isn't in the dining room, and she walks to the front of the house, where Chinasa is entertaining her work colleagues. Expectedly, Zulu isn't there. Ogechi shakes her head in response to Chinasa's raised brow and returns to the house, continuing her search. Nduka, Ikedi, and several guys are in the den watching a football match, and Ogechi starts to panic when she doesn't see Zulu there, worried he might have left without her noticing.

Then she hears the sound of laughter coming from the patio.

With furrowed brows, she walks north in the direction of the sound, and feels her blood boil when she sees Zulu seated next to a light skinned woman - no, girl - her hand on his thigh and her face tilted close to his as they talk. He says something Ogechi can't hear, prompting the girl to laugh again, staring at Zulu like he is a demi-god.

Infuriated, Ogechi walks up to them.

"Chizulukeme, is this where you are?" she demands.

They, Zulu and the girl, look up at her, and while the girl's eyes are wide in her curiosity, Zulu's remain flat.

"Wow, is that your full name?" the girl asks Zulu. "Chizulukeme, I love it!"

Ogechi's nostrils flare and she has to bite her tongue from asking the girl if she can't see that they, the adults there, want to have a conversation. Instead, Ogechi crosses her arms and lifts a brow, her gaze focused on him.

Zulu stares back at Ogechi, spellbound by her heavenly curves in a sleeveless, black dress that hugs every rise and dip of her body. Her chocolate coloured skin is glossy under the patio's dim LED light and his body stirs with longing for this infuriating, arrogant, and stubborn woman.

"Ogechi, meet my friend, Anwuli," he says, trying to keep his face impassive, to keep his raw desire for her from showing on his face.

"Hello, Anwuli," Ogechi answers, not even looking at the girl, her eyes still on him, her mouth downturned, her chin jutted out, and her nostrils flared.

THE MARRIAGE CLASS

His lips curl into a smile as he recognizes the look on her face for what it is. She is jealous. And the realization detonates explosions of delight in the core of his belly.

"Hi," Anwuli answers, an edge in her voice, clearly having picked up on the swirling undercurrents between the pair. "And you are?"

"Ogechi," Zulu answers, a broad smile on his face. "My fiancée."

All the anger seeps out of Ogechi upon hearing him address her with the title that once horribly grated, but which now sounds like a hallelujah verse. Smiling, she reaches for his hand and is relieved, happy, when he accepts it. Without another word, she pulls him to his feet, and leads him out of the patio, leaving his dazed companion staring after them.

But the little girl is the least of her concerns.

"*Achal'ugo*, where are you taking me?" Zulu asks, as they make the turn to the stairway leading upstairs.

Not answering, she ascends the stairs, her hand holding his tight, lest he change his mind. Once upstairs, she pushes him into the first open room, a room reserved for Chinasa's mother when she visits. But she isn't visiting now.

"What are you doing?" Zulu asks, excitement and confusion in his voice as she locks the door and pushes him to the bed, and understandably so, considering she hasn't even let him put his hand on her chest, let alone feel her breast, in all the months they have been together.

She covers his lips with hers in response, in a kiss deeper and more passionate than anything they have ever shared, suddenly wanting him more desperately than she ever has.

Her kiss dissolves any restraint he has tried to exercise and unleashes his basal animal instinct to ravish her, something he has wanted to do from the first moment he laid eyes on her. Flipping her over, so he is now atop her, he pauses to look at her, to take in every detail of her. The part of her lips invites him, the feel of her supple skin beneath his electrifies him, her scent sends him into a heady trance, and as he lowers his head to kiss her, as he touches parts of her body he never had liberty to before, as he peels of her dress and she, his jeans, as their bodies unite the way nature designed them to, as they ride together in natural rhythm, slow and tentative at first, and then fast, demanding, wanton...

He knows he has found heaven.

"I don't like this t-shirt," she says as they lie in the afterglow, her body still tingling.

"Consider it burnt," he chuckles, stroking her bare shoulder. "I will destroy it immediately."

"And these jeans are too tight."

"I'm your blank canvas, *obi'm*. Do with me what you like. Whatever it is you want me to change, just say it, and I will change it," he tilts up her face. "For you, I will do anything."

And looking up at him, she realizes she doesn't want him to change a damned thing.

Omasan & Itse

"I'm sure you're glad the classes are over," Omasan says, getting into bed that night. "No more complaining every Monday and Friday evening."

"It was a waste of time," Itse says, not looking up from his computer perched on his lap as he sits upright on his side of the bed. "Why subject couples to ten classes of things that are all basic, common knowledge."

"Well, not all knowledge is common," Omasan laughs, her eyes falling to his screen. "What are you doing?"

Itse turns to look at her. "Kofo called me this afternoon. He says there might be an opportunity for me at his clinic."

Kofo is their former classmate who now has a thriving medical practice in Houston.

"How can there be an opportunity for you when you're not qualified to practice in America?" Omasan retorts.

"He says he can hire me as an ultrasound technician for the time being, while he works on filing a work permit petition for me with the USCIS," he answers, shrugging. "He says I can take the medical licensing exam after I get there and run that concurrently with this job."

"Ultrasound technician?" Omasan repeats, gaping at him. "Are you even listening to yourself?"

"It's a hundred thousand dollars a year, babe," Itse says, turning to her and grabbing her hands, his eyes wide and dilated in his excitement. "I can start making money while taking the qualifying exams. It's win, win!"

"Do you even know how long it will take Kofo to get the permit for you?"

"He says he can get it in as little as two months, but I need to be there for it to happen."

"And when do you plan to go?"

There is a pause before he finally answers. "Next week. My tourist visa expires soon."

She stares at him for several seconds before bursting into laughter. "Next week, as in first week of July? Boy, quit playing."

THE MARRIAGE CLASS

He looks at her, unsmiling. "I'm not joking, Omasan. I'm serious."

Her laughter fades as she realizes it isn't a joke. "Itse, our wedding is in less than three months. The 24th of September, or have you forgotten? It might sound like a long time to you, but, I assure you, it isn't. And you traveling now, to come back a few days before, just won't work."

"Forget this wedding, Omasan!" he explodes. "I'm talking about what will improve both our lives, you're talking about a wedding. You might feel satisfied with your fat salary here, but in the grand scheme of things, its peanuts! Over there, as an experienced Pediatrician, you can make up to two hundred and fifty thousand dollars a year. Maybe even three. Here in Nigeria, are you even making up to fifty?"

Her eyes narrow. "What are you saying?"

"I'm saying we should both go! Kofo can sort us out while we take the USMLE." His grip on her hands tightens. "Let's leave this place, Omasan. It'll be better for us over there."

"This has nothing to do with better opportunities here or there, does it, Itse?" she asks, her eyes holding his. "If we pack everything up and leave, even when we get there, there will still be excuses about why we shouldn't get married."

He drops his head, sighs, and releases her hands. "Your fixation on marriage is not only irrational, it's frustrating as fuck! I'm talking about us finally making something of ourselves, and you've stuck your fingers in your ears not wanting to hear anything that doesn't have to do with you wearing a big white dress and parading in front of your relatives, letting them know Omasan is married at last!"

"We've made something of ourselves here."

"Speak for yourself, Omasan! Speak for yourself!" he exclaims, throwing his feet off the bed and standing by his bedside, glaring at her. "I barely make three hundred thousand *naira* a month. That's not even up to ten thousand dollars a year! And I had the best fucking result in our class!"

"Second best," she retorts.

He scoffs and smiles, nodding. "But, of course. How could I forget? *You* finished best. *You* have the better job. *You* want to stay here. *You* want to get married. It's all about *you*, isn't it?"

"Do you want to get married, Itse?" she asks, her calm voice belying the rage of emotions warring inside her. "Ever?"

"The truth? I don't know, Omasan," he answers, sighing. "I don't know."

Silence stretches between them for a full minute.

THE MARRIAGE CLASS

"When did we stop loving each other?" she finally asks, breaking the silence.

He shrugs and sighs again. "I think we just allowed ourselves forget how much." He hesitates, before speaking again. "I'm leaving for Houston next week, Omasan. My mind is made up about that. It's left to you to decide whether you'll come or not."

"And if I decide not?" she asks, her eyes searching his.

"Then I guess you'll not."

And in the bedroom they have shared for years, him standing over their bed and her looking up at him…

They both know their relationship is over.

13. THE WEDDING

It's true, the old saying that the journey of life is sometimes ages and sometimes a moment, sometimes difficult and sometimes easy, sometimes complete and sometimes broken, sometimes a firefly and sometimes a star, sometimes an ember and sometimes an inferno. Because, at the start of our marriage class, if anyone had asked me to guess which of the couples wouldn't make it to the finish line, Bianca and the fiancé she had never met would have been top of my list.

But here they are, getting married before the rest of us.

Sitting in the decorated hall at Eagle Club, Surulere, I smile, watching as Bianca and her new husband dance to *Overloading* by the Mavins. In a beautiful confection of white tulle and lace in a mermaid-style dress with a

THE MARRIAGE CLASS

sweetheart neckline, sheer lace sleeves, and floral accents giving the gown a touch of whimsy, Bianca is radiant, her joy palpable. Her husband, Prince, dapper in a fitted navy-blue double breasted suit, is much younger and better looking than I had imagined a man resorting to marrying a woman he'd never seen before, would. The smile on his face is even wider than his bride's and as they dance, as their eyes hold, silently communicating in a language only they understand, they have a connection just as deep as any of the other couples in the class we finished seven weeks ago. Maybe even deeper.

It's amazing how much has changed in seven weeks.

My eyes go to the two couples I am sharing a table with, both of whom missed the last few classes of the marriage course, both of whom I'd also thought wouldn't get to the finish line, but both of whom now looking more in love than ever before. Eric has an arm around Ivie, who is singing along to the song playing, intermittently exchanging glances with him, prompting silly grins from both of them. Today, he is nothing like the abrasive I'd-rather-be-somewhere-else man I remember from our class, his every action this afternoon reflecting the adoration he feels for his fiancée.

"We'd really love for you to come," Ivie had said shortly after we'd taken our seats at the start of the reception, handing me the invitation for their September 3rd destination wedding in Zanzibar. "A charter flight is being arranged for our friends and family, so let me know if you'd like us to book you a seat."

I'd smiled as I accepted the card. "Sounds fantastic. I'll let you know."

Will I want to witness a couple from the same class get married on a beautiful Tanzanian beach a week after my wedding should have happened? Somehow, I think not. But, regardless, I'm happy for them, Eric and Ivie, Ivie especially. They exchange another cheesy grin and this time, he actually blows her a kiss. As she pretends to catch it in the air, giggling as she does, I am glad she got what she wanted in the end.

The other couple on the table, Ogechi and Zulu, seated so close they are almost fused into one, have their arms interlinked and faces touching. She whispers something in his ear which makes him chuckle. To think I once thought the classy and somewhat haughty Ogechi and the rather crude Zulu an incompatible pair. Well, if their new wedding date - brought forward from its initial December date to October 1st, Nigeria's Independence Day - is anything to go by, not only are they in a hurry to walk down that aisle, I guess they're not quite as incompatible as I'd thought. I look at their invitation, which Ogechi gave me shortly after they arrived thirty minutes ago, knowing it is very unlikely I'll be attending the Enugu ceremony either, but happy for them, nonetheless. Zulu whispers something in Ogechi's ear and her face flushes as she laughs. I look away, not having heard what was said but feeling as embarrassed as if I had, uncomfortable by their unabashed PDA. They need to get a room already.

There is a loud roar in the room followed by applause as Prince lifts Bianca and spins her around before setting her

THE MARRIAGE CLASS

back on the floor and tilting her in a deep dip. I smile, clapping along with everyone else. I spot Chioma and A.K. clapping from the table next to ours, and Chioma waves as we make eye contact. She sent me the invitation for their October 15th wedding about a week ago, and, as it is happening here in Lagos, with the ceremony at her family church - incidentally St. Claire's - and the reception at Harbour Point, I just might attend...even if the mere thought of seeing them, or any other couple, exchange vows gives me a sinking feeling in my stomach.

I spot Kris and Bola walk in, and they wave in our direction. With her hand tucked into the crook of his, and their outfits perfectly coordinated, with her in a floor length dress in sparkling red jacquard and him in a black suit with a pocket square the same shade of red as her dress, they are picture perfect as always. Just when I think it is the least risqué I have ever seen her dressed, she turns as she waves at Chioma and A.K., giving me a good view of the cut-out that runs from the nape of her neck all the way to the curve of her bottom, exposing her glossy, dark skin. The woman is sexy for days! The same electricity sizzles between the couple as the first time I saw them, and, from what I hear, their wedding is to hold at the Ikoyi Registry on the 8th of September - a Thursday, for crowd control.

They join Ewa and Sanya where they are seated at a table in front, and I still cannot get over the fact that the much talked about #CheersToTheWellingtons wedding will be happening in Osogbo. I haven't received an invitation, so I reckon it's a ceremony for only close friends and family, which is just as well, as I wouldn't have gone all that way to attend anyway. As Ewa takes yet another selfie when Kris and Bola join them, possibly her hundredth selfie that afternoon, I am certain the wedding is still going to be all over social media. I wouldn't expect less from an 'influencer' with a million Instagram followers. And, no, I'm not being sarcastic.

Far from it.

It's not lost on me that my wedding - our wedding, Raymond's and mine - would have happened before any of theirs.

The events after our breakup were like a tsunami, with frantic visits and calls between both our families. In the end, when Raymond's family decided to respect his reason for the breakup, which was simply that we'd grown apart and had mutually decided it best to end our relationship, my family had no choice but to do the same. And so, the church, vendors, and our extended family were informed, plans were cancelled, and the wedding was officially called off. I knew my sister, Joyce, suspected that, not only was the breakup my fault, it also had something to do with Lucas, and I'd been too ashamed to admit to her she'd be right on both accounts. As for Lucas, I finally blocked him, not just from contacting me but also from whatever hold on my heart he still had. He was bad news and had succeeded in upending my life a second time. But as much as I wanted to blame him for it, I'd been a willing participant. I had a good thing with Raymond, but I'd messed it up. And I have nobody but myself to blame for that.

THE MARRIAGE CLASS

It turns out ours isn't the only relationship that hit the rocks.

As the dance floor opens for guests to join the couple, I notice the heavily pregnant Nkoyo laugh to something the woman she introduced as Offiong, her older sister, says. Her breakup from Nosa is, without a doubt, the most surprising of all, one I never would have predicted.

"We decided it will be better to co-parent," Nkoyo said to me earlier that afternoon, when I couldn't help but ask what had brought about their shocking breakup. "We both want other things."

And other *people*, if the gossip mill is to believed. Ivie says she has run into Nosa with the same woman woman more than once, at Ebeano supermarket. So, it just might be safe to assume he has already moved on.

"Let's stay in touch," Nkoyo said before I left for my table, squeezing my hand in what I interpreted as solidarity, what with us being members of the jilted-almost-at-the-altar club. "I leave for Abuja with my sister in a few days. I'll have the baby there, and," she shrugs and smiles, "see how it goes, I guess."

I'd wrapped my arms around her in an embrace, in empathy...and admiration, wishing I had half her strength and confidence about the future.

As for another couple that didn't make it, Boma and April, I can't say I'm shocked about that. Something about the two of them never meshed, so hearing they have split doesn't surprise me. What is surprising to me, though, is the way he and Omasan have been - dare I say - flirting the whole afternoon. When I heard her loud-mouthed fiancé, Itse, absconded to America, considering he never made his apathy for the entire concept of marriage a secret, even though it was to be expected, I felt deep sympathy for Omasan for wasting nineteen years of her life on the doomed relationship. But watching as she and Boma now converse, with his arm resting on the back of her chair, their bodies angled towards each other, and her laughing at everything that comes out of his mouth, it is obvious they are not having a platonic conversation. As he brushes strands of hair away from her face, tucking them behind her ear, and as their eyes hold as she smiles at him in gratitude, I hope there is more for them than just sex tonight – because they are most definitely having sex tonight – and that this will be the start of something meaningful for them both.

Shortly after, as Ivie and Eric rise to leave, she makes me walk with her.

"Abi, please make sure you come," she says, our arms interlinked as we walk towards the exit. "I know it's hard. I know exactly how you feel. What you need to do is come to Tanzania and make a vacation out it. There at least ten guys coming that I think will be perfect for you."

I laugh, touched by the gesture. Maybe I *will* go to Tanzania after all.

"I'll let you know," I say, embracing her as we get to Eric's Mercedes. "Thank you."

THE MARRIAGE CLASS

I wave as the car pulls away, and as I turn to return to the hall, I see the one person I didn't think I would.

Raymond.

He is walking in the direction of the hall from the car park, and, as if feeling my stare, he looks my way. As our eyes hold, it feels like the last seven weeks never happened.

Like the last three months never happened.

I raise my hand in a feeble wave and he smiles and walks up to me.

"Hi, Abi."

"Hi, Raymond." My voice is raspy and my heart is beating itself out of my chest. "I didn't think you'd be here."

He shrugs. "Sanya forwarded me the invitation, so I thought, why not?" His smile wanes. "You look well. Yellow has always been your colour."

In a bias cut yellow chiffon dress, white Jimmy Choo pumps with a pearl and crystal-embellished bow, my hair slicked back in a ponytail, and makeup in the glossy, bronzy, neutral tones I know compliment me best, I would be lying if I say there isn't some part of me that hasn't hoped for this moment, this moment when I would see Raymond for the first time in seven weeks, this moment when he would tell me how much he misses me and wants me back.

Except he isn't doing that...telling me he misses me or wants me back.

"Thank you," I answer. "You don't look bad yourself."

In a fitted midnight blue *Senator* kaftan, his hair and beard impeccably cropped, he looks perfect.

"Thank you," he says, after which we stand in silence for a while.

"I'm really sorry about everything, Raymond," I finally say, knowing it is the least I can give him - an apology. "I messed up big time, and I'm sorry."

He is quiet for a while before nodding. "I know."

Seeing an opening, I reach for his hand, my eyes holding his, imploring. "I miss you. I love you so much and I would do anything to have you back. Tell me what I have to do to fix this...to fix this us."

He covers my hand with his other one. "You need time, Abi. You never got over that Ibazebo guy, and you need to do the work to get him out of your system."

"But he's already out," I exclaim in protest. "I've blocked him everywhere and even sent a message through Abel, warning him never to contact me again."

"Not just here, Abi," he shakes his head as he taps mine. "But more importantly, here," he taps the left side of my chest, under which my heart is thumping in a frenzy. "You need time to release him here, and completely this time."

THE MARRIAGE CLASS

He smiles. "And I'll be here to support you, if you need me."

I sigh, not knowing whether to be grateful for his offer…or disappointed by it.

"There he is! The elusive Raymond!" comes Ifeyinwa's voice.

Turning around, I am both glad and irritated to see our instructors, Ifeyinwa and Maxwell, as they approach us, happy to see them again but angered by the intrusion.

"You disappeared without any warning," Maxwell says to Raymond, as they shake hands in greeting. Then turning to me, he raises a brow. "And you never did schedule that extra class."

I shrug, not trusting myself to speak, lest I burst into tears.

"Well, we have another round of classes starting in a couple of weeks," Ifeyinwa says, intuitively picking up on what it is I'm not saying. "Maybe you two could repeat the ones Raymond missed?"

Raymond and I look at each other, and a smile curves his lips.

"Maybe next year," he says, his eyes holding mine.

The End

Author's Note

Thank you for coming along with me on this journey with these very different, very indecisive couples. Gosh, they were frustrating, even for me! With this one, I wanted to do something different from my norm, and I hope you loved all their stories just as much as I did. Considering how lengthy my other stories are, I'd thought writing this would be a walk in the park. How wrong I was! Condensing each couple's story without losing its essence was one of the hardest things I have ever had to, some being way harder than others. For two of the couples, I got a little carried away and threw the word count out of the window. I'm sure you can guess which ;-).

All in all, it was a journey I really enjoyed and, as always, I look forward to your comments, messages, and feedback. And no, there will be no spin off stories for any of the couples :-D

Thank you all so much!

About The Author

Investment banker by day, romance writer by night, Adesuwa O'man Nwokedi began writing by accident and what started as a few scribbles for friends has led to 23 titles... and counting. A self-described hopeless romantic, when she's not creating new characters, she's a loving wife and mom of three.

Find her online: https://thefertilechick.ng/

Other Books By Adesuwa

Standalones

Accidentally Knocked Up
Faith's Pregnancy
You Used To Love Me
The Love Triangle
Golibe
Where Is The Love?
Iya Beji
You, Me…Them
A Love Of Convenience
Jaiye Jaiye
Adanna
The Sisters
The One!
Call Me Legachi

The Ginika's Bridesmaids Series

Ginika's Bridesmaids 1: Ara
Ginika's Bridesmaids 2: Isioma
Ginika's Bridesmaids 3: Ife
Ginika's Bridesmaids 4: Ozioma
Ginika's Bridesmaids 5: Ginika
Whatever It Takes (Summer 2023)
Any Love (Christmas 2023)

Malomo High Reunion Series

An Unlikely Kind Of Love
A Complicated Kind Of Love
A Betrayed Kind Of Love
A Broken Kind of Love (Fall 2023)

Printed in Great Britain
by Amazon